Fountain of Christianity
(Chashma-e-Masīḥī)

NAIMAT & RAZIA KHAN
11 HOWSON CRES
EDMONTON, ALBERTA
T5A 4T7

Ḥaḍrat Mirza Ghulam Ahmad of Qadian[as]
The Promised Messiah and Mahdi
Founder of the Ahmadiyya Muslim Jamā'at

ISLAM INTERNATIONAL PUBLICATIONS LIMITED

Chashma-e-Masīḥī
Fountain of Christianity

© Islam International Publications Ltd

First Urdu Edition:
   Qadian, 1906
First English Edition:
   Pakistan, 1970
Present English Edition (New Translation):
   UK, 2008

Published by:
   Islam International Publications Ltd.
   'Islamabad' Sheephatch Lane,
   Tilford, Surrey GU10 2AQ
   United Kingdom

Printed in Great Britain by
Clays Ltd, St Ives plc

Cover Design: Adnan Rashid

ISBN: 1 85372 973 6

CONTENTS

PUBLISHER'S NOTE V

TITLE PAGE OF THE FIRST URDU EDITION XI

AN IMPORTANT ANNOUNCEMENT 1

FOUNTAIN OF CHRISTIANITY 3

EPILOGUE: WHAT IS TRUE SALVATION? 33

SUPPLICATION TO GOD, THE GLORIOUS 71

INDEX OF QURANIC VERSES 73

NAME AND SUBJECT INDEX 74

Publisher's Note

Ḥaḍrat Mirza Ghulam Ahmad, the Promised Messiah[as] and Mahdi, wrote *Fountain of Christianity* in March 1906, in response to a book written by a Christian, in which the gentleman tried to prove that the Holy Quran does not contain any new teachings and that the Holy Prophet[sa] merely copied the narratives from past scriptures–God forbid. The Promised Messiah[as] responds to this objection by, first, raising serious doubts about the authenticity of the Christian Gospels, and then goes on to show how the Holy Quran is a unique and peerless book, how so many of its prophecies have been fulfilled, and how its blessings live on to this day.

In this small book, the author also argues against the doctrines of Trinity and Atonement held by Christians, and shows that these beliefs have nothing to do with the teachings of Jesus himself. In this context, the Promised Messiah[as] also draws out a comparison between the Muslim and Christian teachings of forgiveness and punishment.

The second part of the book, or Epilogue, consists of a profound thesis on the nature of true salvation. The Promised Messiah[as] describes salvation as "The abiding peace and happiness which man, by his very nature, hungers and thirsts for, and which is achieved through personal love and recognition of God, and through a perfect relationship with Him." The Promised Messiah[as] shows that the Christian and Hindu doctrines of salvation have not only failed in this purpose, but are also contrary to the eternal laws and attributes of the Almighty God.

The first translation of this book was done by the late Qadi Abdul Hamid Sahib and was published in 1970. This is a complete new translation prepared by Wakalat Tasnif Rabwah. I am indebted to the following for assisting me in the preparation of this book:

- Raja Ata-ul-Mannan
- Syed Tanwir Mujtaba
- Mirza Uthman Ahmad Adam
- Ahmad Mustansar Qamar
- Tahir Mahmood Mubashar

I would also like to express my appreciation for the help and support given by Maulana Munir-ud-Din Shams, Additional Wakīl-ut-Taṣnīf, who provided the vital link for seeking guidance from Ḥaḍrat Mirza Masroor Ahmad, Khalifatul Masih V[at]. I am also grateful to Ms. Madiha Irfan of Karachi for assisting us in the revision, and to Professor Abdul Jalil Sadiq for proof-reading the final manuscript. May Allah reward them all.

Please note that words in the text in normal brackets () and in between the long dashes—are the words of the Promised Messiah[as]. If any explanatory words or phrases are added by the translator for the purpose of clarification, they are put in square brackets [ ].

The name of Muhammad[sa], the Holy Prophet of Islam, has been followed by the symbol [sa], which is an abbreviation for the salutation *Ṣallallāhu 'Alaihi Wasallam* (may peace and blessings of Allah be upon him). The names of other

Prophets and Messengers are followed by the symbol [as], an abbreviation for *'Alaihissalām* (on whom be peace). The actual salutations have not generally been set out in full, but they should nevertheless, be understood as being repeated in full in each case. The symbol [ra] is used with the name of the companions of the Holy Prophet[sa] and those of the Promised Messiah[as]. It stands for *Raḍi Allāhu 'anhu/'anhā/'anhum* (May Allah be pleased with him/with her/with them). [rh] stands for *Raḥimahullāhu Ta'ālā* (may Allah have mercy on him). [at] stands for *Ayyadahullāhu Ta'ālā* (May Allah, the Mighty help him).

In transliterating Arabic words we have followed the following system adopted by the Royal Asiatic Society.

ا   at the beginning of a word, pronounced as *a, i, u* preceded by a very slight aspiration, like *h* in the English word 'honour'.

ث   *th*, pronounced like th in the English word 'thing'.

ح   *ḥ*, a guttural aspirate, stronger than h.

خ   *kh*, pronounced like the Scotch ch in 'loch'.

ذ   *dh*, pronounced like the English th in 'that'.

ص   *ṣ*, strongly articulated s.

ض   *ḍ*, similar to the English th in 'this'.

ط   *ṭ*, strongly articulated palatal t.

ظ   *ẓ*, strongly articulated z.

ع   ', a strong guttural, the pronunciation of which must be learnt by the ear.

غ   *gh*, a sound approached very nearly in the r *'grasseye'* in French, and in the German r. It requires the muscles of the throat to be in the 'gargling' position whilst pronouncing it.

ق   *q*, a deep guttural k sound.

ئ   ', a sort of catch in the voice.

Short vowels are represented by:

a   for ⸺ (like *u* in 'bud');

i   for ⸺ (like *i* in 'bid');

u   for ⸺ (like *oo* in 'wood');

Long vowels by:

ā   for ⸺ or آ (like *a* in 'father');

ī   for ی ⸺ or ⸺ (like *ee* in 'deep');

ū   for و ⸺ (like *oo* in 'root');

Other:

ai   for ی ⸺ (like *i* in 'site')[*];

au   for و ⸺ (resembling *ou* in 'sound').

Please note that in transliterated words the letter 'e' is to be pronounced as in 'prey' which rhymes with 'day'; however the pronunciation is flat without the element of English diphthong. If in Urdu and Persian words 'e' is lengthened a bit more it is transliterated as 'ei' to be pronounced as 'ei' in 'feign' without the element of diphthong thus 'کے' is transliterated as 'Kei'. For the nasal sound of 'n' we have used the symbol 'ń'. Thus Urdu word 'میں' is transliterated as 'meiń'.[*]

---

[*] In Arabic words like شیخ (Shaikh) there is an element of diphthong which is missing when the word is pronounced in Urdu.

[*] These transliterations are not included in the system of transliteration by Royal Asiatic Society. [Publishers]

viii

The consonants not included in the above list have the same phonetic value as in the principal languages of Europe.

We have not transliterated Arabic words which have become part of English language, e.g., Islam, Mahdi, Quran, Hijra, Ramadan, Hadith, ulema, umma, sunna, kafir, pukka etc.

For quotes straight commas (straight quotes) are used to differentiate them from the curved commas used in the system of transliteration, ' for ع, ' for ء. Commas as punctuation marks are used according to the normal usage. Similarly for apostrophe normal usage is followed.

Chaudhry Muhammad 'Alī
Wakīlut Taṣnīf
Teḥrīk Jadīd
Rabwah
11ᵗʰ October, 2007

Title Page of the First Urdu Edition

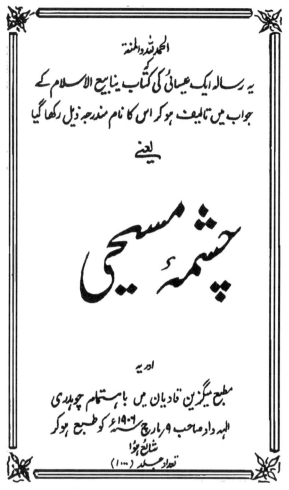

Translation: By the Grace and Mercy of Allah, this book has been written in response to the book *Yanābī-ul-Islam*, written by a Christian, and it has been named *Fountain of Christianity*.

Printed in Magazine Press, Qadian, under the supervision of Chaudhary Aladād Sahib, and published on 9th March, 1906.

Number of copies: 1000

بِسْمِ اللّٰهِ الرَّحْمٰنِ الرَّحِيْمِ

نَحْمَدُهٗ وَنُصَلِّیْ عَلٰی رَسُوْلِهِ الْکَرِیْمِ[1]

An Important Announcement
Pertaining to the Prophecy about the Earthquake

Rouse yourselves friends
For another earthquake is in sight;
God is again going to manifest
His power and His might.

Be sure that the earthquake
You witnessed in February
Was a mere jolt
To warn and to make you wary.

O unheeding people!
With the water of your eyes
Try to quench the fire
That is about to rain from the skies.

Why should earthquakes not come
When goodness and piety wane;
Even a Muslim today
Is only a Muslim in name.

Did they accept me for fear of Him?
Did they give up their malevolence?
Nay, to hear their vilification
Seems to be the purpose of my existence.

They call me an infidel,
An antichrist, and a man of sin;
The chance of their accepting me
Truly and sincerely, is slim.

---

[1] In the name of Allah, the Gracious, the Merciful. We praise Allah and invoke His blessings upon His noble Messenger. [Publishers]

Wherever you may look
People are steeped in prejudice and ill will;
One only has to ask,
They will ascribe [to me] every fault and every ill.

Having abandoned the Faith*
They have fallen for the world;
No matter how I admonish
They will not heed my word.

My heart nearly stops
When I see the Faith* in adversity;
But the Hand of God
Is about to restore its** tranquillity.

Now will you have
A taste of His ire;
This calamity shall spread
Far and wide its empire.

The Faith* will now be helped
By the hand of death;
Or one of these days, O friends,
It would draw its last breath.

The Faith,* for which a whole world
Was once ready to die,
Today the wretchedest man
Is ready to vilify.

Announcement by:
Mirza Ghulam Ahmad of Qadian
The Promised Messiah
March 9ᵗʰ, 1906

---

* Islam [Publishers]
** My heart's [Publishers]

بِسْمِ اللّٰهِ الرَّحْمٰنِ الرَّحِيْمِ

نَحْمَدُهٗ وَنُصَلِّیْ عَلٰی رَسُوْلِهِ الْكَرِیْمِ[2]

Fountain of Christianity[3]

The book I am about to write is titled *Chashma-e-Masīḥī*. There was really no need for me to write about the beliefs of the Christian clergymen, for, in these days, their own renowned scholars in Europe and America have taken this task upon themselves—one which should have actually been performed by us. Nonetheless, they are doing a wonderful service by revealing the truth about Christianity.

I have recently received a letter from an ill-informed Muslim in Bānsbareilly, in which he has expressed serious concern about *Yanābī-ul-Islam,* a book written by a Christian. It is unfortunate that most Muslims, because of their apathy, do not study my books and are completely ignorant of the blessings that God has bestowed upon me. Furthermore, ignorant Mullahs have also created a barrier between us by repeatedly calling me a kafir. This is why Muslims are not aware that the days have passed when the deception

---

[2] In the name of Allah, the Gracious, the Merciful. We praise Allah and invoke His blessings upon His noble Messenger. [Publishers]

[3] The title *Chashma-e-Masīḥī* does not mean 'Fountain of the Messiah[as]', because the Messiah's teachings, which have been lost to the world, did not teach the prevailing doctrines. These doctrines have been invented by the Christians themselves, and this is why this book has been named 'Fountain of Christianity'. [Author]

3

Fountain of Christianity

and deceit of the Christians could work, and that we are now in the sixth millennium since the birth of Adam—the time when the Divine dispensation (*Silsilah*) was destined to triumph. This is the last battle[4] between light and darkness, in which light shall be victorious and darkness shall be vanquished. Again, it was really not necessary for me to write about the outdated beliefs of the Christian clergy, but I had to do it on the insistence of the above-mentioned gentleman. May God bless this effort and let this book be a source of guidance for the people. Āmīn.

Remember, we hold Jesus[as] in great esteem, and regard him as a Prophet of God.[5] We are also averse to the kinds of objections raised against him that have recently been published by the Jews. My aim is only to show that just as the Jews attack Jesus and his Gospel out of sheer prejudice, in much the same way the Christians attack the Holy Quran and the Holy Prophet[sa]. Christians should not have followed the misguided ways of the Jews, but it is a rule that when people are unable to attack a religion on the ba-

---

[4] The word 'battle' must not be taken to mean a battle fought with swords or guns, for God has now forbidden this kind of Jihad. This form of Jihad was destined to be abolished in the time of the Promised Messiah[as], as foretold by the Holy Quran. *Ṣaḥīḥ Bukhārī* also contains the Hadith يَضَعُ الْحَرْبَ* which refers to the Promised Messiah[as]. [Author]

* He [the Promised Messiah] shall put an end to war. [Publishers]

[5] Whatever unpleasant things have come forth from my pen regarding Jesus[as] are only by way of counteraccusation. I have done no more than to reproduce the words of the Jews. If only the Christian clergymen could be civil and God-fearing and would stop abusing our Holy Prophet[sa], the Muslims would respond with twenty times greater cordiality. [Author]

Fountain of Christianity 5

sis of truth and justice, many of them resort to slanderous attacks. This is also what the author of *Yanābī-ul-Islam* has done. The love of this world is the cause of all such evil, otherwise Islam is the only heavenly religion which continues to manifest fresh blessings. It is only through the pure fountain of Islam that man is led to the Living God; and the artificial 'God', who lies buried in Srīnagar (Mohallah Khanyār), Kashmir, can be of no avail to anyone. I will now turn to the gentleman from Bareilly and commence this book. وَاللّٰهُ الۡمُوَفِّقُ [It is Allah Who guides to the right path].

Mirza Ghulam Ahmad of Qadian
The Promised Messiah
1ˢᵗ March, 1906

بِسُمِ اللّٰهِ الرَّحْمٰنِ الرَّحِيْمِ

نَحْمَدُهٗ وَنُصَلِّیْ عَلٰی رَسُوْلِهِ الْکَرِیْمِ وَ نَبِیِّهِ الْعَظِیْمِ[6]

اَلسَّلَامُ عَلَیْکُمْ[7] It was with a heavy heart that I read your letter, which you wrote after studying the book *Yanābī-ul-Islam,* authored by a Christian. I am surprised that you have begun to harbour doubts about Islam on account of the falsehood and deceit spread by people whose God is dead, whose religion is dead, whose book is dead, and who are themselves dead for they lack the spiritual eye. اِنَّا لِلّٰهِ وَ اِنَّا اِلَیْهِ رَاجِعُوْنَ[8] You must remember that these people have not only interpolated the books of God, but have surpassed every other people in falsehood and fabrication in order to promote their faith. Since they do not possess the light which descends from heaven in support of the truth, and distinguishes a true religion through repeated testimonies, they are forced to employ all kinds of deceit, fabrication and fraud to alienate people from the living faith—Islam.

---

[6] In the name of Allah, the Gracious, the Merciful. We praise Him and invoke His blessings upon His noble Messenger and exalted Prophet.
[Publishers]
[7] Peace be on you. [Publishers]
[8] An expression of regret or sorrow. Literally: 'We belong to Allah, and to Him shall we return.' [Publishers]

Brother! These are black-hearted people who do not fear God. They are trying, day and night, to make people love darkness and forsake the light. I cannot understand how you could be influenced by the writings of such people. They are, in fact, worse than the magicians who had turned ropes into serpents in the presence of Prophet Moses[as], but since he was a Prophet of God, his staff swallowed up all their serpents. The Holy Quran is like-wise the 'staff of God' which continues to swallow up snakes made of ropes, and the day is coming—it is indeed at hand—when they shall all disappear without a trace.

The author of *Yanābī-ul-Islam* has tried to prove that the Holy Quran has been copied from certain accounts or books, but his effort is nothing compared to the effort made by a learned Jew to determine the authenticity of the Gospels. He has established, in his own estimation, that the moral teachings of the Gospels have been taken from the Jewish scripture Talmud and certain other books of the Israelites, and that this act of plagiary has been so bla-tant that whole paragraphs have been copied word for word. The scholar has proved that the Gospels are a col-lection of stolen material, and has gone so far as to prove that the 'Sermon on the Mount'—in which Christians take such pride—has been copied verbatim from the Talmud. He has shown that the text has also been copied from various other books, and has thus astonished many people. European researchers are also taking a keen interest in this research. I recently came across a book written by a Hindu in which he, too, had tried to prove that the Gospels have

Fountain of Christianity 9

been taken from the teachings of Buddha, and he cited Buddha's moral teachings to establish this point. The story about the devil, who took Jesus[as] from place to place to tempt him, is also prevalent among the Buddhists. Everyone is, therefore, entitled to believe that the story has been copied in the Gospels with minor alterations. It is an established fact that Jesus[as] came to India and his grave is to be found in Srīnagar, Kashmir, as I have proved with categorical evidence. And in this context, the detractors are further justified to believe that the existing Gospels are merely a sketch of Buddhism. The evidence in this regard is so overwhelming that it can no longer be concealed.

Another incredible fact is that the ancient book of Yūz Āsaf (which most English scholars believe to have been published before the birth of Jesus[as]), and which has been translated in all European countries, is so similar to the Gospels that many of their passages are identical. The parables used by the Gospels are also found word for word in this book. Even if the person reading it were so ignorant as to be practically blind, he would still be convinced that the Gospels have been borrowed from the same book. Some people, including some English scholars, believe that this book belongs to Gautama Buddha, and that it was originally in Sanskrit and was later translated into other languages. If this is true, the Gospels would lose all their credibility and Jesus[as] would be considered a plagiarist in all his teachings—God forbid. The book is available for everyone to see. My own opinion, however, is that this book is Jesus'[as] own Gospel which was written during his journey to India. I have proved with many arguments that it is indeed the Gospel of Jesus[as], and is purer and holier than the other Gospels. The English scholars who consider this book to be that of Buddha, call Jesus[as] a plagiarist by implication, and thus they dig their own grave.

It should also be remembered that the clergy's collection of scriptures is completely worthless and even embarrassing. They whimsically declare some books to be divine and others to be forged. They judge these four Gospels to be authentic and the rest—about fifty-six of them—forged. But this belief is based on mere guesswork and speculation, rather than on any concrete evidence. They have had to make these decisions by themselves, for there is a marked discrepancy between these and the other Gospels. Researchers, however, believe that it is not possible to determine which of them is actually forged and which is not. This is why, on the occasion of King Edward's coronation, the Church fathers of London presented him with the books which they presume to be forged along with the four Gospels, all bound in one volume. I possess a copy of this Bible. Now, if these books had really been forged and were unholy, would it not be sinful to bind the holy and the unholy in a single volume? The fact is that these people are unable to say with any degree of conviction whether any of these books are authentic or forged, and everyone goes by their own opinion. Out of mere prejudice, they declare those Gospels to be fabricated which are in accord with the Holy Quran. Hence they have declared the Gospel of Barnabas to have been forged because it contains a clear

Fountain of Christianity
11

prophecy about the Prophet of the Latter Days[sa] [the Holy Prophet]. Sale, in his commentary, has related the story of a Christian monk who was converted to Islam after reading this Gospel. Remember, these people declare a book to be false or fabricated for either of these two reasons:

1. If an account or a book contradicts the current Gospels.

2. If an account or a book has some similarity with the Holy Quran. Some mischievous and black-hearted people first try to establish the principle[9] that these books are fabricated, and then claim that the Holy Quran contains stories taken out of them, and in this manner they try to deceive the ignorant.

The fact is that only Divine revelation has the authority to prove the truth or falsity of past scriptures. Any account confirmed by Divine revelation has to be true, even though some ignorant ones declare it otherwise. Similarly, the account which Divine revelation rejects, has to be false, even though some people declare it to be true.

To think that the Holy Quran is made up of such well-known accounts, tales, books or gospels, is the height of ignorance and something to be ashamed of. Is there anything wrong with a book of God being in agreement with some past accounts? Many truths of the Vedas, which were not even known at the time, are to be found in the

---

[9] Christianity does not only allow the use of falsehood and imputation in support of the faith, but considers this practice to be worthy of divine reward. See the teachings of Saint Paul. [Author]

12   **Fountain of Christianity**

Holy Quran, but can we conclude from this that the Holy Prophet[sa] had studied the Vedas? The Gospels that have now become available—thanks to the printing press— were not known to anyone in Arabia, and the people of that land were simply unlettered. If there happened to be an odd Christian among them, he was not likely to know much about his own religion.[10] It is therefore despicable to think that the Holy Prophet[sa] plagiarized from these books. The Holy Prophet[sa] was unlettered and could not even read Arabic, let alone Greek or Hebrew. It is now upon our opponents to produce any manuscript of that time from which these accounts are supposed to have been taken. If the Holy Quran contained material copied from other sources, the Christians of Arabia, who were bitter enemies of Islam, would at once have cried out that it has been taken from their own accounts.

Remember, the Holy Quran[11] is the only scripture in the world that proclaims itself to be a miracle. It forcefully asserts that its prophecies and narratives are from the realm

---

[10] Reverend Pfander has admitted in his book, *Mīzān-ul-Ḥaq,* that the Christians of Arabia were also like savages and were quite ignorant. [Author]
[11] The Holy Quran claimed that it was a unique and miraculous book, and it challenged anyone who considered it to be the word of man to come forward and prove it, but no opponent took up the challenge. The Gospels, on the other hand, were declared plagiarized by the Jews at that very time [when they were written], nor have they ever claimed that man cannot produce anything like them. Therefore, the Gospels may be suspected of having been plagiarized, but not the Holy Quran, for it claims that no man can ever produce such a book and the silence of the opponents has proved the truth of this claim. [Author]

Fountain of Christianity 13

of the unseen, it contains prophecies about the future down to the Last Day, and that it is a miracle in respect of its eloquence and beauty of expression. It would have been easy for the Christians of that time to produce the books from which passages were supposedly copied in the Holy Quran, thus dealing a severe blow to Islam. But now they only cry over spilled milk. It is unthinkable that the Christians of Arabia would have kept quiet despite being in possession of books—whether genuine or forged—from which they suspected the Holy Quran of having copied certain material. Thus there can be no doubt that the Holy Quran is totally composed of the revealed word of God, and that this revelation was a great miracle, for, no one could produce anything like it.

Just consider, can a person dare to give such a challenge to the whole world, while being a plagiarist and having cooked the whole thing up on his own, and knowing full well that this knowledge has not come to him from the unseen, rather he has stolen it from such and such books, and to think that no one should be able to accept his challenge and expose him!

The fact is that the Christians are extremely annoyed with the Holy Quran, for it has destroyed the very basis of their religion. It has refuted the concept of deifying a human being, shattered the doctrine of the cross, and proven beyond all doubt that the teachings of the Gospels—which the Christians are so proud of—are extremely flawed and ineffective. It was, therefore, only natural for their egoistic passions to have been aroused, and their imputations [against the Holy Quran] are quite understandable. The example of a Muslim who wishes to convert to Christianity is like a person who, having been born from his mother's womb and having attained maturity, wishes to return to her womb and become a sperm once more. I wonder what the Christians are so proud of! If they have a 'God', he is the one who died long ago and lies buried in Mohalla Khanyār, Srīnagar, Kashmir. And if he has any miracles to his name, they are no greater than those of other Prophets, indeed Prophet Elijah showed greater miracles than he ever did. In the eyes of the Jews, Jesus[as] showed no miracles at all, and it was all deception and trickery.[12] And if we look at his prophecies, most of them turned out to be false. Will some padre tell us if the twelve disciples were indeed given twelve thrones in Paradise, as they had been promised! And will someone tell us if, in keeping with his prophecy, Jesus[as] got the Kingdom of the World, for which—by the way—weapons were also acquired. And did Jesus[as] descend from heaven in those very days, as he had promised? Let me tell you that there can be no question of his descent, for he never went to heaven in the first place. European scholars also concur with this belief. The fact is that Jesus survived the

---

[12] This statement of the Jews is corroborated by Jesus[as] himself, for he says in the Gospels, "An evil and adulterous generation seeketh after a sign, and there shall no sign be given unto it..." If Jesus[as] had shown miracles to the Jews, he would surely have referred to them on this occasion. [Author]

Fountain of Christianity 15

crucifixion in a state of near death, and then secretly fled to Kashmir through India where he [ultimately] died.[13]

The teachings of the Gospels—regardless of whether they have been accused of plagiarism—emphasize only the human faculties of forbearance and forgiveness, and discard the rest. Everyone can understand that nothing which has been given to mankind by Divine Omnipotence is without a purpose, and every human faculty has a function. Just as forgiveness and forbearance is considered a great virtue at certain times and occasions, so is retaliation, revenge and retribution considered a commendable moral quality at other times and on other occasions. Neither forgiveness, nor punishment is always desirable. This is what Allah teaches us in the Holy Quran:

---

[13] Those, who call themselves Muslims and yet believe that Jesus[as] ascended to heaven in his physical body, utter an absurdity against the Holy Quran which affirms Jesus' death in the verse فَلَمَّا تَوَفَّيْتَنِي* , and precludes the possibility of a man ascending to heaven in the verse قُلْ سُبْحَانَ رَبِّيْ هَلْ كُنْتُ اِلَّا بَشَرًا رَّسُوْلًا** . How ignorant of them to hold a belief in contradiction to the Word of God! There can be no greater folly than to translate the word *tawaffā* as 'being lifted to heaven with one's physical body'. Firstly, in no lexicon do we find the word *tawaffā* being translated as such. Moreover, since the verse فَلَمَّا تَوَفَّيْتَنِي speaks about the Day of Judgement, and this is what Jesus[as] will have to say for himself on that day, it follows that the Last Day will arrive but Jesus[as] will not have died, for he will have presented himself before God in his physical body before he could ever be made to suffer death. To misinterpret the Holy Quran thus is to surpass even the Jews in the art of interpolation! [Author]

* …when Thou didst cause me to die…—Al -Mā'idah, 5:118 [Publishers]

** Say, my Allah is Holy, I am not but a human being and a Messenger of God.—Banī Isrā'īl, 17:94 [Publishers]

16   **Fountain of Christianity**

جَزٰٓؤُاۡ سَيِّئَةٍ سَيِّئَةٌ مِّثۡلُهَا ۚ فَمَنۡ عَفَا وَاَصۡلَحَ فَاَجۡرُہٗ عَلَی اللّٰہِ[14]

'The recompense of an injury is an injury the like thereof; but whoso forgives and his act brings about reformation,[15] his reward is with Allah.'

This is the teaching of the Holy Quran. The Gospel, on the other hand, teaches unconditional forgiveness at all times, and thus tramples upon all sense of expediency on which the social structure is based. It only emphasizes the growth of one branch of the 'tree' of human ethics, and completely disregards all the others.

But, strangely enough, Jesus[as] did not act upon his own moral teachings. He cursed the fig tree when he found it to be barren, while he exhorted others to pray. And while he taught others not to call anyone a fool, he himself went to the extent of calling the Jewish elders misbegotten, hurling abuses at them in every sermon and calling them foul names. A teacher of morals must first exhibit those morals in himself. Could such a flawed teaching, which Jesus[as] himself did not follow, be from God?

The only pure and perfect teaching is that of the Holy Quran, which nourishes all human faculties. It does not emphasize any one aspect, rather it teaches a judicious

---

[14] Al-Shūrā, 42:41 [Publishers]

[15] The Holy Quran does not approve of that forgiveness which serves no good purpose, for it only corrupts human morals and creates disorder in society. The Holy Quran only sanctions that forgiveness which results in reformation. [Author]

Fountain of Christianity 17

exercise of both forgiveness and chastisement. In truth, the Holy Quran is a reflection of the Divine law of nature which we witness all around us. It stands to reason that there should be harmony between God's word and action. The action of God, as we see it in this world, must necessarily be the basis for the word of God contained in His True Book—not that His Action should point to one thing and His word to another. With regard to His action, we observe that forgiveness is by no means the rule, and that He also inflicts upon the wrongdoers various kinds of punishments, which have been mentioned in earlier scriptures as well. Our God is not only Forbearing, but He is also most severe in His wrath. The True Book, therefore, is the one which conforms to His law of nature, and the true Divine Word is that which does not contradict His action. We have never observed God to be continually forbearing and forgiving towards His creatures and never punishing them. Even today God has warned the wicked people through me and has told of a powerful and terrible earthquake which will destroy them; and the plague has not yet subsided either. Do you not remember what happened to the people of Noah[as] and what befell the nation of Lot[as]?

Do understand that the essence of the Shariah is تَخَلَّقُ بِاَخْلَاقِ اللّٰهِ , which means to adopt the attributes of the Exalted and Glorious God. This is the highest perfection a soul can attain. The desire to acquire morals greater than God's, is sheer blasphemy, and amounts to an attack on His holy attributes.

You should also consider that it is God's eternal and established law that He forgives in response to repentance and penitence, and hears the prayers of His righteous servants which are offered by way of intercession. But we never observe in the Divine law of nature that 'A' hits his own head with a stone and this cures the headache of 'B'. We are, therefore, at a loss to understand how people can acquire inner purification through the suicide committed by the Messiah. Is there any law or philosophy which can make us understand how the Messiah's blood could have cleansed the inner impurities of other people? Our observation is, in fact, opposed to this principle, because, until the time when the Messiah decided to commit suicide, we find an element of righteousness and godliness among the Christians. After the crucifixion, however, their carnal passions burst forth like a river which breaks its banks and inundates the land.

There is no doubt that even if this suicide on the part of the Messiah was deliberate, it was quite needless. If he had, instead, spent his life in preaching and exhortation, he would have done a lot of good for God's creation. But this act did not serve them in any way. Yes, if the Messiah had indeed come back to life after his suicide, and had ascended to heaven before the very eyes of the Jews, they would surely have believed in him. But, as things stand, the Jews, and all reasonable people, consider the Messiah's ascension to be no more than a fable.

The doctrine of Trinity is also rather peculiar. Has anyone

Fountain of Christianity 19

ever heard of something being permanently and perfectly 'three' and 'one' at the same time? Or that one God should be as perfect as three Gods? Christianity is indeed a strange religion, which errs at every step.

And, not content with all this darkness, it has set a seal on all future revelation. According to the Christian belief, it is no longer possible to correct the errors contained in the Gospels through fresh revelation, because they believe Divine revelation to be a thing of the past. Everything now comes to rest upon individual opinion which can never be free from ignorance and darkness. It is, in fact, impossible to count the absurdities that are to be found in the Gospels, like the deification of a humble man, proposing the Messiah's crucifixion as a penalty for sins committed by others, banishing him to hell for three days, and declaring him to be God while attributing weakness and falsehood to him at the same time! There are many passages in the Gospels which prove that the Messiah[as]— God forbid—was guilty of falsehood. For example, he promised a certain thief that he would break fast with him in heaven that very day, but, in breach of his promise, he went to hell and stayed there for three days. It is also written in the Gospels that the devil took the Messiah from place to place in order to tempt him. Is it not strange that the Messiah, being 'God', was not immune to satanic temptations, and that the devil had the cheek to tempt Him at all! This is quite a unique philosophy! If the devil had indeed visited the Messiah, it would have provided him an excellent opportunity to show him to the Jews, as they were strongly opposed to his claim of Prophethood. The sign of the true Messiah, which had been mentioned in the Book of Malachi, was that the Prophet Elijah[16] would return to the world before his coming, but since Prophet Elijah did not return, the Jews have called Jesus[as] a liar and an impostor to this day. And the Christians are at a loss to counter this argument of the Jews.

The Jews also say that the account of the devil calling upon the Messiah is a sign of insanity, and that many insane people experience such hallucinations and nightmares. An English scholar has said that this visitation of the devil means that the Messiah received satanic revelations on three occasions, but remained unmoved by them, and that in one of them he was urged to renounce God and submit himself wholly to Satan. How strange that the devil subdued 'the Son of God' and inclined him towards the world! And Jesus even suffered death, despite being called 'God'! Does God ever die? And if it was only a man who had died, then why do they claim that 'the Son of God' gave up his life for the sake of mankind? What is

---

[16] In those days, the Jews were awaiting the second advent of the Prophet Elijah and his descent from heaven, exactly as our simple-minded maulawīs these days are waiting for Jesus[as] to descend from heaven. Jesus[as] interpreted the prophecy of Prophet Malachi differently, but the Jews do not believe him to be a true Prophet to this day because Elijah[as] never descended from heaven. And they have met hell due to this belief. Today Muslims are the victims of the same delusion, in complete imitation of the Jews. This has nevertheless served to fulfil a prophecy of the Holy Prophet[sa]. [Author]

Fountain of Christianity 21

more, despite being 'the Son of God', Jesus does not know the hour of Resurrection, and his statement to this effect is recorded in the Gospels. How absurd for God not to know the hour of Resurrection! That may be a distant event, but he was not even aware that the fig-tree he was heading for was barren!

Returning to the main discussion, let me briefly say that no Divine revelation can be attacked merely on the basis of its similarity, or partial-similarity, to a past book or account, even if that book or account is considered to be fictitious. When the Christians label a book as 'historical' or 'revealed', they do so without any substantial proof, and none of their books are free from the stains of doubt and suspicion. It is quite probable that the books they call forged or fabricated are not fabricated at all, and the ones they consider to be authentic may, in fact, be fabricated. A book of God cannot be subject to such likes and dislikes. Their labelling of certain books as fictitious is not something that has been proven by judicial inquiry, nor is it on the basis of established evidence that they declare a book to be authentic. It is all based on speculation and conjecture, which cannot be the criterion for judging a book of God. The true criterion is whether the book proves its Divine origin through God's law of nature[17]

---

[17] The Holy Quran is the only book in the world that has shown God and His attributes to be in accord with the same law of nature which is the result of God's 'action' in this world and is imprinted in human nature and conscience. The God of the Christians is confined to the leaves of the Contd...

and through powerful signs. Our Lord and Master, the Holy Prophet[sa], showed more than three thousand miracles and made countless prophecies. But we do not have to refer to these miracles of the past, for, a great miracle of the Holy Prophet[sa] is that, while the revelation of all the Prophets have come to an end, and their miracles are a thing of the past, and their followers are empty-handed but for a few fictitious tales, the revelation of the Holy Prophet[sa] has not ended, nor have his miracles, for they continue to be manifested in his perfect followers through the blessing of their obedience to him. This is why Islam is the living religion and its God is the Living God. Today, I, His humble servant, am here to bear testimony to this. Thousands of signs, testifying to the truth of the Prophet of God and the Book of God, have so far been manifested through me, and God blesses me with His pure word almost every day. Think carefully, how can we prove that a religion is actually from God while there are thousands of religions in this world that attribute themselves to Him? Should a true religion not have some distinction? The fact that a religion is rational cannot be a proof of its being from God, for man, too, can speak of rational things. And the 'God' who is only a creation of man's own reason is no God at all; God is He

---

Gospel, and anyone whom the Gospel has not reached remains ignorant of Him. But no thinking man can be unaware of the God presented by the Holy Quran. The True God is the one Who has been presented by the Quran and testified by human nature as well as the law of nature. [Author]

Who manifests Himself through powerful signs. A truly Divine religion must possess signs of being from God, and it must possess the Divine seal to prove that it has indeed come from Him, and this religion is none other than Islam.

It is through this religion that God, Who is hidden and invisible, comes to be known, and it is to the followers of this religion that He manifests Himself. He supports the true religion and manifests His existence to the world through it. Religions that are only based on tales are hardly distinguishable from idol-worship, for they are devoid of the spirit of truth. If God is still Living as He was before, and if He still speaks and hears as He did in the past, then why should He have observed such silence in this age as if He did not exist? If He does not speak today, then surely He does not hear either, which means that He practically does not exist. Hence the true religion is that which testifies that God hears and speaks even in this age. In the true religion, God Himself informs about His existence through His dialogue and communion.

Recognition of God is not something easy, and it is not for the sages and philosophers of this world to try to find Him. The study of heavens and earth can only prove that there 'should be' a Creator of this highly ordered universe, but it cannot prove that He actually exists. And the difference between 'should be' and 'is' is quite obvious. The Holy Quran is the only book that proves God's existence as a fact. It does not only enjoin the recognition of God, but actually reveals Him to us. There is no other book under the firmament which provides proof of that Hidden Being.

What is the aim of religion? It is only that man should have full faith in the existence of God and in His perfect attributes, and then deliver himself from his carnal passions and develop a personal love for Him. This, in fact, is the Paradise, which will find various manifestations in the Hereafter. To remain unmindful of the True God, and to keep away from Him, and not to love Him truly, is the Hell which will reveal itself in diverse forms in the Hereafter. The purpose of religion is to attain full faith in the existence of God and to love Him completely.

Let us now see which religion and which book provides the means to achieve this purpose. The Gospel gives a point-blank answer: The door to Divine converse and dialogue is closed, the path to achieving conviction is forever barred, everything is confined to the past, and there is nothing for the future. It is indeed strange that while God can hear in this age, He cannot speak! Is there any consolation in the belief that He could hear and speak in the past but now He only hears and cannot speak? What is the use of a 'God' who loses his powers with the passage of time, just as man loses his faculties with old age? And what is to be gained from a 'God' who cannot forgive the sins of his servants until he has been flogged, spat in the face, imprisoned for days, and then crucified? We are tired of this 'God' who was overwhelmed by the Jews—a helpless people who could not even hold on to their own kingdom. On the other hand, the God Whom we consider to be the True God is He Who appointed as His Messenger a poor and helpless man from Mecca, and showed a manifestation of His power and glory to the whole world at that very time, so much so, that when the Persian Emperor sent his soldiers to arrest the Holy Prophet[sa], the Omnipotent God told him to inform them, "Tonight my God has killed your god."

Just consider, in the first instance we have a man who claimed to be God, but ended up being arrested by a Roman soldier and thrown into jail, and his night-long prayers remained unanswered. In the second instance, we have a man who claimed only to be a Messenger, but God annihilated even the kings who stood up against him!

The saying یارغالب شوکہ تاغالب شوی [Be the friend of the mighty, so that you may prevail], is of great value for a seeker after truth. What is the use of a religion that is dead, and of what value is the book that is dead, and what can we gain from a God who is dead? I swear by Him, in Whose hand rests my life, that I am honoured with the most certain and definite Divine conversation, and I am honoured with it almost every day. The God, to Whom Jesus had said, 'Why hast Thou forsaken me?', has not forsaken me. There have been many attacks on me, as there had been on the Messiah, but my enemies were frustrated in every one of them. A conspiracy was even hatched to have me executed, but, unlike the Messiah, I was not be crucified. Instead, my God saved me at the time of every trial, demonstrated great miracles for my sake, and helped me with His mighty hand. Through thousands of signs, He has proved to me that the True God is He Who revealed the Holy Quran and sent the Holy Prophet[sa]. I do not at all consider Jesus to be superior to me in these matters. Just as the Word of God was revealed to him, so is it revealed to me; and just as he is said to have shown miracles, so have I been granted miracles, though in greater numbers. All this honour has been conferred upon me solely by virtue of being a follower of the Prophet whose spiritual station and high standing is largely hidden to the world, and he is none other than Muhammad, the Chosen One[sa].

It pains me to hear ignorant people say that Jesus[as] is alive in heaven, whereas it is in the Holy Prophet[sa] that I see the signs of life. It is through him that we have found the God Whom the world does not know; it is through him that the door of Divine revelation—which remains closed to other people—has been opened for us; it is through him that we have been shown miracles which other people relate only as tales; and we have found his status to be so high that there is no status beyond it. How strange that the world should be unaware of all this! People ask me how I could have claimed to be the Promised Messiah. Let me tell them that, through complete obedience to the Holy Prophet[sa], one can attain a status even higher than that of Jesus[as]. The blind call this heresy, but I say: How do you know what heresy is when you are yourselves devoid of faith and heresy is inside you? Had you understood the meaning of the verse:

Fountain of Christianity　　　　　　　　　　　　　**27**

اِهۡدِنَا الصِّرَاطَ الۡمُسۡتَقِیۡمَ ۬ صِرَاطَ الَّذِیۡنَ اَنۡعَمۡتَ عَلَیۡهِمۡ [18]

you would not have uttered such things. Do you consider it heresy to acquire the perfections of just one Prophet, while God promises that, through perfect submission to the Holy Prophet[sa], you can acquire the perfections of all the Prophets?

Do pay attention, for it is possible to recognize a true religion which is from God, and the true religion is the one that leads to Him. While other religions lay stress on human efforts to find God—as if they were doing Him a favour by doing so—in Islam God manifests His own existence by pronouncing اَنَا الۡمَوۡجُوۡدُ [I do exist!] in every age, and He has manifested Himself to me in this age. Peace and blessings be on that Prophet a thousand times, for through him we have recognized the True God.

I am sorry to say that you only expose your ignorance when you express doubts about the statement that Mary[as] was the sister of Aaron. Scholars have written a lot to counter this objection. Why should it surprise you if, by way of metaphor or for some other reason, God has declared Mary[as] to be the sister of Aaron? The Holy Quran has repeatedly mentioned Aaron[as] as a Prophet who lived in the time of Moses[as], and has mentioned Mary[as] as the mother of Jesus[as], who was born some fourteen hundred years later. Do you wish to say that God was unaware of these facts, and that He has made a mistake by declaring

---

[18] Al-Fātiḥah, 1:6-7 [Publishers]

Mary[as] to be the sister of Aaron[as]? How vile are the people who raise such objections and then rejoice upon them! Is it not possible that Mary[as] might have had a brother named Aaron? 'Absence of knowledge about something does not prove that it does not exist.'

These people do not look into their own hearts, and do not see that the Gospel is itself the target of countless objections. Just imagine how strong the objection that falls upon Mary[as] is, for she had pledged to serve the Temple all her life and not to take a husband, but when her pregnancy became apparent in its sixth or seventh month, the elders of the community married her off to a carpenter by the name of Joseph, while she was still with a child. And a mere couple of months after going into his house, she gave birth to a son who was named ʿĪsā or Jesus. The first objection is that, if this was indeed a miraculous conception, why did they not wait until the child was born? The second objection is that while Mary[as] had pledged to serve the Temple for the rest of her life, why was this pledge broken and why was she withdrawn from the Sacred House and given in marriage to Joseph, the carpenter? The third objection is, why was she married to Joseph during her pregnancy, when it is strictly forbidden in the Torah, and when Joseph himself was unhappy with the marriage and he already had a wife living with him. Those who are against polygamy are perhaps unaware of Joseph's first marriage. A critic, therefore, has every right to conclude that this marriage was affected because the elders of the community suspected Mary[as] of having conceived illegitimately. But we,

Fountain of Christianity 29

in the light of the teachings of the Holy Quran, believe that the conception was a manifestation of God's power, for He wished to give the Jews a sign of the Day of Resurrection. When thousands of insects are born by themselves during the rainy season, and Adam[as] was also born without parents, it is no proof of Jesus' eminence if he, too, was born in the same manner. In fact, being born without a father deprives a person of certain faculties. It was on the basis of this suspicion that Mary[as] was married off, otherwise there was no reason to marry of a woman who had been dedicated to the service of the Sacred House. The unfortunate thing is that this marriage occasioned a lot of mischief and the Jews were able to spread rumours of an illegitimate relationship. This is the objection that really needs to be answered, and the objection about Mary[as] being the sister of Aaron is no objection at all. The Holy Quran never says that Mary[as] was the sister of Aaron, the Prophet. It only mentions the name 'Aaron' and there is no mention of 'Prophet'. It was a custom among the Jews to adopt the names of Prophets as a blessing. Therefore, it is by no means inconceivable that Mary[as] had a brother named Aaron, and it is sheer folly to question this statement.

And where is the harm if the story of Aṣḥāb-e-Kahf [the Companions of the Cave] is also found in the earlier books of Jews and Christians, even if we suppose that these accounts are fictitious? Remember, their religious and historical books, and even their revealed ones, are all cloaked in darkness. You do not know how Europe is bemoaning these books, and how good people are

30   **Fountain of Christianity**

instinctively being drawn towards Islam, and how books
are being written in its support. This is why many people
from countries like America have joined my Jamāʻat.
Falsehood cannot remain hidden forever! Why would
Divine revelation need to copy extracts from such books?
These people are blind and so are their books. Only those
who do not at all fear God can make such objections
against the Holy Prophet[sa], for it is obvious that the people
of the Peninsula in which the Holy Quran was revealed had
virtually no knowledge of Christian and Jewish books, and
the Holy Prophet[sa] was himself unlettered. If such an objection can be raised against the Holy Prophet[sa], then just
imagine the sort of objections that would be raised against
Jesus[as], who learnt the Torah word for word from a Jewish
scholar, and read all the books of the Jews such as the
Talmud, and whose Gospel is replete with passages from
Talmud and the Old Testament! The Gospel is, in fact, so
susceptible to all kinds of suspicions that we would not
have believed in it had the Holy Quran not commanded us
to do so. What a pity that there is nothing in the Gospel
which is not to be found in earlier scriptures in exactly the
same words. Why, then, should it be considered unreasonable and outrageous if the Holy Quran has collected
the scattered truths and verities of the Bible in one place?
And how can you say that Divine revelation cannot be the
source of all the Quranic accounts, while it has been established with clear and categorical signs that the Holy
Prophet[sa] was a recipient of Divine revelation, and the
blessings of his true Prophethood continue to be mani-

Fountain of Christianity 31

fested even to this day? Why should one allow Satanic ideas to enter one's mind and think that—Heaven forbid—an account contained in the Holy Quran has been taken from some earlier writing or book? Do you doubt the existence of God, or is it that you do not believe Him to be the All-Knowing?

As I have already said, the Jews and Christians have no solid grounds for declaring one book to be authentic and another inauthentic, for none of them is a witness to the authenticity of the one, and none of them has caught the forger of the other. I have the testimonies of European scholars themselves to this effect. They [Jews and Christian] are a blind people, devoid of the light of faith. The state of the Christians is even more deplorable, for their knowledge of science and philosophy has been of no avail to them. They deny the very existence of Heaven but, at the same time, believe Jesus[as] to be sitting there!

If earlier Jewish scriptures are considered to be true, they do not bear out the Prophethood of Jesus[as]. For example, according to the Book of Malachi, Elijah[as] had to reappear before the coming of the true promised Messiah—who Jesus[as] claimed to be—but Elijah[as] has not appeared to this day. This was a weighty argument put forward by the Jews, but Jesus[as] was unable to give a satisfactory answer. The Holy Quran has indeed done a great favour to Jesus[as] by affirming his Prophethood!

As for the doctrine of the Atonement, it, too, was rejected by Jesus[as] when he likened himself to Jonah[as] who had remained alive in the belly of a fish for three days. If Jesus[as] had died on the cross, what resemblance would there be between him and Jonah[as]? The comparison clearly proves that Jesus[as] did not die on the cross, and, like Jonah[as], he had only become unconscious.

Then there is *Jesus' Ointment*, which is recorded in nearly all books of medicine as having been prepared for the wounds that Jesus[as] had suffered on the cross.

---

[19] This much should suffice if anyone is listening. [Publishers]

Epilogue: What is True Salvation?

Before concluding this book, I feel that I should write something about the nature of true salvation, because salvation is the ultimate objective which followers of every religion hope to attain. But, unfortunately, most people remain unaware and unmindful of the true meaning of salvation. To the Christians, salvation means deliverance from the accountability of sin, but this cannot be its true meaning, for it is quite possible that a person may not be guilty of committing fornication, nor of theft, nor of bearing false witness, nor of murder, nor of committing any other sin which he knows of, and yet he might be deprived of the benefits of salvation. Salvation, in fact, is the abiding peace and happiness which man, by his very nature, hungers and thirsts for, and which is achieved through personal love and recognition of God, and through a perfect relationship with Him—a relationship in which the fire of love is ablaze on both sides.

But people very often try to attain this happiness through other means which only serve to increase their pain and misery in the long run. Most people tend to seek eternal happiness in the carnal pleasures of the world. They indulge day and night in drinking and fulfilling their sensual desires, and end up suffering from all kinds of fatal diseases. They succumb to trauma, paralysis, Parkinson's

34   **Fountain of Christianity**

disease, *kuzzaz,*[20] intestinal ulcer, ulcer of the liver, or
they die as a consequence of shameful diseases such as
syphilis and gonorrhoea. Since their energies have been
prematurely sapped, they fail to complete their natural
lifespan, and it ultimately dawns upon them that things
which they thought would bring them joy and content-
ment had, in fact, brought about their ruin. Some others
think that happiness lies in worldly prestige, rank and of-
fice; they, too, remain unaware of the real object of their
life and die with regret. Then there are those who keep
accumulating wealth in the hope that it will bring them
true happiness. But ultimately they also have to leave behind all their accumulated wealth, and have to drink the
cup of death in great regret and sorrow.

The question before a seeker after truth is, how to achieve
that true happiness which will bring him eternal peace and
happiness. One of the signs of a true religion is that it
leads man to this true happiness. Through the guidance of
the Holy Quran, we arrive at the subtle truth that everlasting happiness lies in the recognition of God, and in pure
and perfect and personal love for Him, and in absolute
faith, which causes the heart to become restless like a true
lover. These are a few words, but volumes would not suffice to explain their meaning adequately.

Remember, there are a number of indications for the true
recognition of God. One of them is that no imperfection is

---

[20] A disease arising from cold, as a consequence of which the patient
trembles to death. (Lane) [Publishers]

Fountain of Christianity 35

attributed to His Omnipotence, His Oneness, His Knowledge, and His other excellences and attributes. If we consider Him—Who controls every particle and commands all the legions of souls and the forces of heaven and earth—to be imperfect in His power and wisdom, the physical and spiritual worlds would at once come to a stand still. If, God forbid, we were to believe that all particles and their powers, and all the souls and their faculties have come into being on their own, it would follow that the Knowledge, Oneness and Omnipotence of God are all imperfect. If particles and souls are not His creation, there is no reason why we should believe that God has knowledge of all that is hidden in them. If there is no conclusive proof of His Omniscience, and the proof is, in fact, to the contrary, we will have to conclude that, like us, God is also unaware of the true nature of things, and that His knowledge does not encompass their innermost secrets.

For example, if we have prepared a medicine with our own hand, or if a syrup or a tablet or an extract has been made with our own prescription and before our very eyes, we will have complete knowledge of that medicine, and we will know all its ingredients as well as the proportion in which they have been added, and we will also know the purpose for which it has been made. But if we have an extract or potion or pill which is unknown to us and whose ingredients we cannot separate, we would surely know nothing about it. In the same way, if we believe God to be the Creator of all particles and souls, we will also have to accept that He possesses all knowledge about them and their hidden faculties and powers, for He is their Creator, and the creator cannot be ignorant of what he creates. But if God is not the Creator of these faculties and powers, there can be no way to prove that He has any knowledge about them. It is sheer temerity to say that He has this kind of knowledge without giving any argument to prove it.

As against our argument—that a creator has to have knowledge of his creation—do you have anything to prove that God knows about the hidden qualities of things which [you believe] He has not created with His own hands, and while they are not even part of His own Being so that He should know them just as a person knows himself? According to the Ārya belief, all things are their own gods, and are eternal and self-existent, and are so independent of the Parmeshwar [God] that it would make little difference to them even if He were dead. And it is obvious that if they did not need Him for their creation, they will also have no need of Him for their continued existence.

Two of God's names are حَيّ (*Hayyī*) and قَيُّوم (*Qayyūm*). *Hayyī* means the Living One Who also gives life to others. *Qayyūm* means the Self-Subsisting One Who also sustains His creation. Only such things can benefit from God's attribute *Qayyūm* which have already benefited from His attribute *Hayyī*, for He supports the things that He has created, and not those which His hand has not even touched. Therefore, only he who believes God to be *Hayyī*, i.e., the Creator, can believe Him to be *Qayyūm*, i.e., One Who sustains His creation. But he who does not believe God to be the Creator has no right to believe that He is the sustainer. Here the concept of sustenance implies that everything would cease to exist if His sustenance was withdrawn. Things which have not been created by Him can obviously not be dependant upon Him for their sustenance. And if they do, they surely owe their creation to Him as well. In short, both these attributes of God, *Hayyī* and *Qayyūm*, are interrelated and can never be separated from each other. If those who believe that God has not created the particles and souls were to employ their thought and reason, they would have to admit that God is also not their Sustainer, i.e., they cannot say that particles and souls are dependent upon God for their sustenance, because only those things depend upon His sustenance as have been created by Him. Why would something require His sustenance when it has no need for His creation? Such a claim will, therefore, have to be considered baseless.

I have just stated that if we consider particles and souls to be eternal and self-existent, it will be impossible to prove that God has knowledge of their hidden and intrinsic powers and faculties. To say that He does have knowledge about their hidden faculties and powers because He is their Parmeshwar [God] is a mere claim which is neither supported by any argument, nor corroborated by any evidence, nor established on the basis of a relationship between the Creator and His creation. In fact, He is not even their Parmeshwar. How can he be their Parmeshwar of particles and souls when He is not their Creator? And on

38 Fountain of Christianity

what basis can we apply this possessive noun between them? A possessive noun can be used in the sense of ownership, for instance, when we say, 'Zaid's slave', we understand that there should be some reason for this ownership. But we do not see why independent things, that have possessed their powers and faculties from eternity, should be considered as being owned by Parmeshwar. In the second instance, the possessive noun denotes relationship, for instance, one might say, 'Zaid's son'. But if particles and souls are not related to God as His creation, there will be no justification for such a relationship either. There is no doubt that for such 'independent' souls, the existence of Parmeshwar is of no use, nor will they have anything to lose by His non-existence. In this situation, salvation—which the Ārya Samāj refer to as *muktī*—becomes impossible to attain, for it wholly depends upon the personal love for God which He has created in the very nature of the souls. If souls have not been created by Parmeshwar, how can they love Him by their very nature? And Parmeshwar could not have placed His love in their nature afterwards, because natural love is something that has to be eternally inherent in them and not something that was created later on. This is what God refers to in the Holy Quran when He says: [21]اَلَسۡتُ بِرَبِّکُمۡ قَالُوۡا بَلٰی i.e., I asked the souls, "Am I not your Creator?" And the souls replied, "Yes, indeed." The meaning of this verse is that the soul contains in its very nature the testimony that God is its Creator. The

---

[21] Al- Aʿrāf, 7:173 [Publishers]

Fountain of Christianity 39

soul, being God's creation, loves Him naturally and instinctively. The same thing has been referred to in another verse where Allah says, فِطْرَتَ اللّٰهِ الَّتِيْ فَطَرَ النَّاسَ عَلَيْهَا[22] i.e., It has been ingrained in human nature that it will always seek after the One and Only God, and will not find true happiness in anything apart from its union with Him, i.e., God has created in human soul a desire that it shall not find true comfort and tranquillity in anything other than its meeting with God. If this desire is inherent in human soul, then one has to acknowledge that soul is indeed a creation of God, and it is He Who has placed this desire within it. And since this desire is most certainly present in human soul, it proves that God is its Creator.

Love obviously grows stronger between two beings according to the closeness of their mutual relationship. For instance, a mother loves her child and a child loves its mother because it was born out of her blood and was fostered in her womb. If souls are not bound to God in the relationship of the Creator and the created, and they are eternal and self-existing, then there is no reason why their natures should be imbued with such love for Him. And if their nature is devoid of love for Parmeshwar, they will obviously never attain salvation.

The real source and essence of salvation is man's personal love for God, which leads to his union with Him, because a lover cannot remain separated from his beloved. Since

---

[22] Al-Rūm, 30:31 [Publishers]

40   Fountain of Christianity

God Himself is Light, His love produces 'the light of salvation'. The love which is ingrained in human nature
draws the love of God, and then God's personal love
gives extraordinary strength and enthusiasm to man's personal love, and the union of the two results in the state of
'annihilation' (*Fanā*) and culminates in the light of 'immortality with God' (*Baqā Billāh*). The fact that the
meeting of the two loves necessarily leads to 'annihilation
in God' and the body (which is only a veil) is totally con-
sumed, and the soul becomes wholly submerged in Divine
love, can be illustrated with the example of a man who is
struck with lightning. The fire falls upon him from
heaven, and its powerful attraction draws the fire that is
within him, and this results in the annihilation of the
body. In the same way, spiritual annihilation also requires
two kinds of fires: the heavenly fire and the inner fire of
man. The meeting of both these fires creates a state of 'annihilation (*Fanā*), without which the spiritual journey
remains incomplete. This is the state of 'annihiliation'
(*Fanā*) where the journey of the spiritual wayfarers comes
to an end, and it is the limit beyond which human endeavour cannot go. After reaching the point of *Fanā*, man is
granted the status of 'eternity' (*Baqā*) as a gift and a favour. This is what the following verse points to:

صِرَاطَ الَّذِيْنَ اَنْعَمْتَ عَلَيْهِمْ 23

Briefly stated, it means that anyone who attains this sta-

---

23 Al-Fātiḥah, 1:7 [Publishers]

Fountain of Christianity 41

tion, attains it as a reward and through God's grace, and not as a recompense for his endeavour.[24] This is the culmination of man's love for God, through which he attains the eternal life and is delivered from death. Immortality is not the privilege of anyone but God. He alone is Eternal. Therefore, out of all mankind, this eternal life is attained only by the one who cuts himself off from all other loves, and, having 'annihilated' himself in his love for God, receives from Him a share of eternal life by way of reflection (*zill*). It would not be proper to call such a man 'dead', for he has come to life through God. Truly dead are those who die while they are estranged from God.

Hence, those who believe that all souls possess an eternal life, without having developed personal love for God and without having 'united' with Him, are completely faithless. The truth is that nothing has any existence without God. He alone is called 'Living'; and it is only when the souls of the righteous come under His 'shadow' and immerse themselves in His love that they are given true life, and this life can never be attained without 'uniting' with Him. In the Holy Quran, Allah has described the disbelievers as 'dead', and regarding the inmates of Hell He says:

---

[24] Since man, on account of his human weakness, cannot perform actions which will entitle him to unlimited favours, and without these he cannot reach true salvation, God takes pity on his weakness after he has tried to the best of his ability, and helps him through with His grace, and gives him, as a gift, the reward of His union which was given to righteous people before him. [Author]

إِنَّهُ مَن يَأْتِ رَبَّهُ مُجْرِمًا فَإِنَّ لَهُ جَهَنَّمَ لَا يَمُوتُ فِيهَا وَلَا يَحْيَى[25]

i.e., he who comes to his Lord a sinner, for him is Hell; he shall neither die therein nor live.

He will not die because the purpose of his creation was to be eternally subservient to his Lord, and for this reason his continued existence is necessary. But he will not be alive either, for true life is attained only through union with God. The true life is salvation itself, it cannot be had without the love of God and without union with Him. Had the people of other faiths been aware of this philosophy, they would never have claimed that all souls are eternal, self-existing and blessed with true life. This kind of knowledge only comes from heaven, and only heavenly people truly comprehend it while the world is unaware of it.

Returning to the initial point, let me reiterate that the source of eternal salvation lies in union with God, and only he who drinks the water of life from this fountain attains true salvation. But this union cannot come about without true recognition (*Ma'rifat*), true love, true sincerity and true faith. The first sign of true recognition is that one should not attribute any flaws to God's knowledge. I have just shown that those who believe particles and souls to be eternal and self-existing, do not consider God to have perfect knowledge of the unseen. This is also the reason why the erring Greek philosophers, who considered the souls to be eternal, believed that God did not

---

[25] Ṭā-Hā, 20:75 [Publishers]

Fountain of Christianity

possess knowledge of minute things, for, when the souls and particles are eternal and self-existing, and when they are not indebted to God Almighty for their existence, it cannot be argued that God is cognizant of their infinitesimal qualities and hidden attributes. It is obvious that while we know every hidden detail and every latent quality of things that we have ourselves created, it is not possible to claim the same precise knowledge regarding other things, and there is always the possibility of error in our knowledge about them. So, those who consider souls and particles to be eternal and self-existing are bound to admit that their Parmeshwar does not have such knowledge about souls and particles as befits His majesty, for His knowledge should be as perfect as Himself. But if someone still asserts [in the context of this belief], that Parmeshwar does possess such knowledge, he should give a clear proof of it instead of just making verbal claims.

If souls are taken as eternal and self-existing, it would mean that they also have a separate abode of which they have permanent possession, and that Parmeshwar lives somewhere else, there being no connection between them. These people cannot give any reason as to why all particles and souls—despite being eternal and self-existing—should be subservient to Parmeshwar? Did this come about as a result of some war, or did the souls themselves consider it expedient to surrender themselves to Him? They believe that, despite being Kind and Just, Parmeshwar neither shows mercy nor acts with justice, and He refuses to grant eternal salvation to the souls in order to cover up His weaknesses, because if He admits the souls into eternal salvation, they will all at one time have attained salvation and saved themselves the trouble of being unceasingly sent back to the world. But since Parmeshwar wants the universe to continue—so that He might go on ruling it—He does not wish to admit any soul into eternal salvation, to the extent that even if a soul becomes an Avatar, or a Rishi, or a Siddh, He still keeps throwing it back into the cycle of transmigration. But can we ascribe to the Kind and Omnipotent God such meanness that He should take pleasure in tormenting His creatures and refuse to ever grant them eternal peace? No, such meanness can never be attributed to the Pure and Holy God. But, it is unfortunate that teachings which ascribe meanness to Him are to be found in the books of the Christians as well. They believe that whoever refuses to accept Jesus as God will be thrown into the everlasting Hell. But this is not the teaching God Almighty has given us. We have been taught that the disbelievers, after suffering chastisement for a time, will ultimately partake of God's mercy, as described in the following Hadith:

يَأْتِيْ عَلٰى جَهَنَّمَ زَمَانٌ لَيْسَ فِيْهَا اَحَدٌ وَ نَسِيْمُ الصَّبَا تُحَرِّكُ اَبْوَابَهَا

i.e., a time will come upon Hell, when there will be no one in it; and its doors shall be moved to and fro by the morning breeze.

Likewise, it is written in the Holy Quran:

Fountain of Christianity **45**

اِلَّا مَا شَآءَ رَبُّكَ ۚ اِنَّ رَبَّكَ فَعَّالٌ لِّمَا يُرِيْدُ [26]

i.e., the inmates of Hell will abide in it forever, but God shall deliver them from it when He so wishes, for He can do what He pleases.

This teaching is completely in accord with God's perfect attributes, for His attributes are both *Jalālī* [possessing awe and glory] and *Jamālī* [possessing beauty, kindness]. He is the One who causes the wound, and He is the One who applies the soothing balm.[27] It is unreasonable and contrary to the perfect attributes of God to think that, after He has condemned someone to Hell, His awe-inspiring attributes should continue to manifest themselves forever while the attributes of compassion and forgiveness should remain dormant, and His benevolence and mercy should become forever suspended. On the contrary, we know from what God says in His Book that the inmates of Hell will dwell in it for a long time—which has metaphorically been called 'eternity' in view of human weakness—but the attribute of mercy and kindness shall thereafter manifest itself and God shall put His Hand into Hell and take out as many as it will hold. This Hadith also shows that salvation will be granted

---

[26] Hūd, 11:108 [Publishers]

[27] It is in itself unreasonable to argue that man should be condemned to everlasting punishment, and that, in accordance with God's eternal existence, the inmates of Hell should also remain in it forever. God, too, has something to do with their failings, for it is He Who created weakness in their nature. The inmates of Hell, therefore, deserve leniency due to the weakness which God Himself has put in their nature. [Author]

46   Fountain of Christianity

to all,[28] for the Hand of God is infinite like Himself, and no one will be left out of it.

Remember, just as the stars appear one after the other at their appointed times, so do Divine attributes manifest themselves at the appropriate time and occasion. Sometimes man is under the shadow of God's attributes of glory and *Istighnā* [being Independent and Besought of all], and sometimes he is under the influence of His attributes of mercy and compassion. This is what the verse كُلَّ يَوْمٍ هُوَ فِى شَأْنٍ [29] alludes to. It is, therefore, a folly to think that after the guilty people have been thrown into Hell the attributes of kindness and mercy will become suspended and will forever cease to manifest themselves. God's attributes can never be suspended. The attribute of love and compassion is a basic Divine attribute, and it is the mother of all other attributes. It is this very attribute that sometimes manifests itself in the form of awe and glory so as to bring about man's reformation, and once the reformation has taken place, it assumes its original form and endures forever as a gift from God. God is not like an ill-tempered person who is fond of tormenting others. He is not cruel to anyone, rather men are cruel to themselves. All salvation lies in His love, and all torment lies in forsaking Him.

---

[28] Salvation does not mean that everyone will enjoy the same status. Those who accept God in this world, and immerse themselves in His love, and take their stand on the right path, have special honours in store for them, which shall not be given to others. [Author]

[29] Al-Raḥmān, 55:30 [Publishers]

This, then, is the concept of God held by the Ārya Samāj, and it leads us to believe that whoever has been honoured in the sight of God—whether he be an Avatar, a saint, or someone to whom the Vedas have been revealed—his status is not permanent, and that he will be dispossessed of the seat of honour a thousand times. He may be the beloved of Parmeshwar at one time, and might enjoy a position of nearness to Him as an Avatar, a Rishi or whatever, but at another time, in the eternal cycle of transmigration, he might be reduced to a mere insect or a worm, and he will never attain eternal salvation. He lives in this world in fear of death, and continues to live in fear of the torment of transmigration ever after.

This, in short, is their treatment of God. While they declare souls and particles to be equal to Him by virtue of their eternal and self-existing nature, they also declare Parmeshwar to be so mean and miserly that—despite His power and Omnipotence—He refuses to grant eternal salvation to anyone.

The true nature of the Vedic teachings about human chastity becomes obvious from their doctrine of *Neug*, which, briefly stated, is that an Ārya may allow his wife to sleep with a stranger for the purpose of procuring an offspring, and she may continue to do so everyday until she has eleven children from this 'pious' relationship.

I mentioned this only in passing, I will now return to the point that, in view of the Ārya doctrine, their Parmeshwar cannot be considered the Knower of the Unseen, nor do the Āryas have any argument to prove that He possesses such knowledge.

In the same way, the Christians also do not consider God to be the Knower of the Unseen, for they consider Jesus[as] to be God, and he himself is known to have confessed that he—being the 'Son of God'—was not aware of the hour of Resurrection. The inference from this is that the hour of Resurrection is not known to God.

The second requirement of true *Ma'rifat* [recognition of God] is to realize that God has absolute power, but in this respect also the Ārya Samāj and the Christian padres ascribe shortcomings to Him. The Ārya Samāj do this by denying that Parmeshwar is the Creator of souls and particles; and they do not believe that He has the power to admit even a single soul into everlasting salvation.[30]

The Christian clergy also do not believe their God to be

---

[30] We have every reason to be grateful to our God, Who always keeps manifesting for us the signs of His power, so that our faiths may be continually refreshed. For instance, He revealed to me on four different occasions that the Punjab would experience a terrible earthquake. Accordingly, a strong earthquake struck on the morning of Tuesday, 4th April, 1905. This was during the spring season, and the Powerful God thereafter revealed to me that several more earthquakes would also strike in spring. Exactly as He had foretold, a terrible earthquake struck right in the middle of spring on 28th February, 1906, and it shook the Manṣūrī Hills so forcefully that the people nearly lost their senses. At the same time, parts of America also experienced an earthquake which destroyed many cities. The True God, therefore, is He Who even today reveals to us the signs of His power. Thousands of prophecies that were granted to me through Divine revelation have also been fulfilled. [Author]

Fountain of Christianity 49

All-Powerful, for their God was beaten, imprisoned, whipped and crucified by his opponents. If He had indeed been All-Powerful, He would never have borne such disgrace. Had He been all that powerful, He would not have thought of killing Himself for the sake of bringing salvation to His creatures. It is indeed shameful to speak of 'power' in the context of this 'God' who remained dead for three days. It is also strange that while 'God' remained dead, His creatures continued to live without Him!

As for their concept of the Oneness of God, the Ārya Samāj believe all souls and particles to be partners with their Parmeshwar by virtue of their self-existence. They also ascribe the creation and continuous existence of these particles and souls to their own inherent ability; and this clearly amounts to associating partners with God.

As far as the Christians are concerned, they are clearly opposed to the Oneness of God,[31] for they believe in three

---

[31] The Quran teaches us that, just as God has created the souls, so has He the power to annihilate them; and that man's soul attains immortality only through His grace and bounty, and not through its own effort. This is the reason why those who are perfect in their love and obedience to God, and bow themselves before Him with perfect faith and perfect certainty, are given a perfect life which is exclusive to them. Their natural senses and instincts are greatly sharpened, and their nature is blessed with a Light which causes extraordinary spiritual power to be born in them. And all the spiritual powers which they are given in this world are greatly enhanced after death. By virtue of their God-given affinity with the Almighty, they are raised to Heaven, and this is what is known as *Raf'a* in the Shariah. But those who do not believe, and do not have pure affinity with God, are not given this life or these attributes. These people, therefore, fall under the Contd...

'Gods'—the Father, the Son, and the Holy Ghost. Their explanation, that they believe 'three' to be 'one', is really quite absurd. No sane person can be expected to accept such flawed logic, especially when the three Gods are considered to be permanently self-existing and each is thought to be a complete God in Himself. What kind of arithmetic is it that shows them to be one, and where is it taught? Is there any logic or philosophy that can explain how beings which are permanently three can be counted as one? It is only a deception to argue that this is a mystery which human reason cannot understand, for human reason clearly understands that if there are three perfect Gods, they will have to be 'three' and not 'one'. This doctrine has not only been rejected by the Holy Quran, but also by the Torah. The latter, which was given to Moses[as], contains no mention whatsoever of the Trinity. If it had contained such a teaching, the Jews could never have forgotten it, for they were enjoined to stick to the teaching of the Unity of God to the extent that each and every Jew was commanded to memorize it, to inscribe it on the door of his house, and to teach it to his children. In addition, Prophets of God continued to appear among the Israelites and gave them the same teaching. It is, therefore, inconceivable that, despite such great emphasis and coming of so many Prophets, the Jews could have forgotten the teaching of Trinity and re-

---

category of the 'dead'. If God had not been the Creator of the souls, He would never have used His power to show such distinction between the believers and the disbelievers. [Author]

Fountain of Christianity 51

placed it with the teaching of the Oneness of God, which they continued to teach their children and which continued to be reiterated by hundreds of Prophets. This would go against all reason and logic. I have myself made an effort in this regard, and have asked some Jews to tell me on oath whether or not the teaching given to them in the Torah was that of the Trinity? They wrote back to me—and I have preserved their letters—that the Torah does not contain even a hint of the Trinity; and that the Torah's teaching about God is the same as that of the Holy Quran. Hence, we can only pity the people who have become so obstinate about a doctrine that is to be found neither in the Torah, nor in the Holy Quran, nor even in the Gospels! Nowhere do the Gospels even hint at the Trinity, they only speak of the One God Who is without peer. Some eminent and even hostile clergymen have had to admit that the Gospels do not teach the doctrine of the Trinity. How then did this concept find its way into the Christian faith? According to Christian scholars, this doctrine was borrowed from the Greeks, who believed in three gods just as the Hindus believe in Trimurti (three idols). When Paul turned his attention to the Greeks,* he wished to please them so that they could convert to Christianity. With this in mind, he introduced into the Christian faith the concept of 'the three persons of the Godhead', to mirror the Greek concept of three gods, despite the fact that Jesus[as] himself had never thought of such a thing. Like all Prophets, his teaching

---

* 'Jews' in the Urdu original seems to be a misprint. [Publishers]

about God was simple and categorical, viz., God is One and He has no partner.

It is important to realize that the religion which is championed as 'Christianity' is, in fact, the religion of Paul and not that of Christ, for the latter never taught the doctrine of the Trinity. As long as he lived, he only taught the Oneness of God and His being without partner. After he died, his brother James—who was his successor and a holy man—also taught the Oneness of God. But Paul unjustly opposed him and started preaching contrary to his true teachings, and went to the extent of creating a new faith. He set his followers against the Torah and taught them that there was no need for the Law after the Messiah's Atonement, and Christians did not need to follow the Torah because the Messiah's blood was enough to wipe away their sins. Another abomination which he introduced into this religion was that he made the eating of swine lawful, whereas the Messiah had declared swine to be an unclean animal. This is what he meant when he used the expression, 'Do not cast pearls before swine'. While he compared the holy teachings to pearls, he likened unclean and impure people to swine. The truth is that the Greeks used to eat the flesh of swine, just like the people of Europe today, and it was in order to win their hearts that Paul declared it to be lawful, even though the Torah had forbidden it forever and had even forbidden anyone to touch it. Thus Paul is responsible for all the ills that are found in this religion.

Jesus[as] was a humble and selfless person who did not even

Fountain of Christianity 53

want to be called 'good'; but Paul made him 'God'. It is written in the Gospels that someone said to Jesus "O Good Master!", but he said, "Why callest thou me good?" And how wonderfully do the words which he uttered at the time of the crucifixion testify to his belief in the Oneness of God. With the utmost humility, he had cried, *Eli, Eli, lama sabachtani?*, "My God! My God! Why hast Thou forsaken me?" Can any reasonable person believe that he who supplicated to God with such humility, and considered Him to be the Lord and Master, could himself have claimed to be God?

The truth is that those who have a relationship of personal love with God are often made to use some metaphoric expressions regarding themselves which ignorant people use to prove their divinity. More such expressions have been used for me than they were for the Messiah.[32] For example, Allah addressed me and said:

---

[32] I once saw in a *kashf* [a vision experienced while awake] that I created a new earth and a new heaven, and then I said "Now, let us create man." [When this *kashf* was made public], the ignorant mullahs raised a great tumult and accused me of claiming to be God. What the *kashf* actually meant was that God would bring about such a great change through me that heaven and earth would become new, and true people would be born. Similarly, God once said to me, اَنْتَ مِنِّیْ بِمَنْزِلَةٍ اَوْلَادِیْ اَنْتَ مِنِّیْ بِمَنْزِلَةٍ لَّا یَعْلَمُهَا الْخَلْقُ i.e., "You are to Me like an offspring, and your relationship to Me is such that the world knows nothing of it." The mullahs became wild at this and asked if there could be any more doubt about my being a kafir, and they completely forgot the verse, فَاذْکُرُوااللهَ کَذِکْرِکُمْ اٰبَآءَکُمْ * [Author]
* Remember Allah as you remember your forefathers.—Al-Baqarah, 2:201
[Publishers]

يَا قَمَرُ يَا شَمْسُ اَنْتَ مِنِّى وَ اَنَا مِنْكَ

i.e. "O Moon! O Sun! You are from Me and I am from you." Anyone can construe these words to mean whatever he likes, but their true meaning is that God first made me the 'Moon', for, like the Moon, I was manifested through the True Sun; thereafter, He became the 'Moon', for the light of His Glory shone through me and will continue to do so.

So, Jesus'[as] brother James, son of Mary[as], was a righteous man. He followed the Torah in everything, believed God to be One without any partner, considered the flesh of swine to be unlawful, faced the Holy Temple while praying—as was the custom of the Jews—and considered himself a Jew in everything, with the exception of his belief in the Prophethood of Jesus[as]. Paul, on the other hand, turned people against the Holy Temple. God's vengeance ultimately overtook him and he was crucified by the king, and thus he met his end. But Jesus[as] was saved from crucifixion because he was true in his claim and he was from God. Paul, on the other hand, was hung from the stake for he had forsaken the truth.

It is also worth noting that as long as Jesus[as] lived, Paul was his sworn enemy, and, according to Jewish chronicles, he only turned to Christianity after Jesus' death because he had some selfish desires which the Jews did not fulfil. Therefore, in order to avenge himself, he became a Christian and pretended that Jesus[as] had appeared to him in a vision. He first sowed this unholy plant in Damascus, and this is the place where 'Pauline Trinity'

Fountain of Christianity 55

was born. The Hadith in which it is said that the Messiah who is to come will descend towards the East of Damascus alludes to the same thing. It means that the doctrine of the Trinity will come to an end with his coming, and people's heart will be inclined towards the Oneness of God. The appearance of the Messiah in the East signifies that he will become victorious, for when the light dawns it overcomes darkness.[33]

If Paul was indeed meant to appear as an Apostle after the Messiah, the latter should have foretold something about him. This was necessary because Paul had bitterly opposed Jesus[as] throughout his life, and had contrived to harm him in every way. How could such a person be trusted after Jesus' death, unless he himself made a clear prophecy that, although Paul has been my bitter enemy and has done me great harm, he will become an Apostle and a holy man after I am gone. This was all the more important because Paul gave a teaching that was against the Torah, and declared eating the flesh of swine to be lawful, and even abolished the Divine commandment regarding circumcision, although it had been greatly stressed in the Torah and all Prophets—including the Messiah himself—had been circumcised. He also replaced the teachings of the Torah regarding the Oneness of God with the teaching of the Trinity, and declared it unnecessary to follow the

---

[33] Please note that Qadian, the place where I reside, is located exactly to the East of Damascus. The Holy Prophet's[sa] prophecy has, therefore, been fulfilled in this age. [Author]

commandments of the Torah, and turned away from the Holy Temple. It was, therefore, essential that some prophecy should have been made regarding this person who played such havoc with the Mosaic Law. But in the absence of any such prophecy in the Gospel, and in view of his hostility towards Jesus[as] and his opposition to the timeless commandments of the Torah, is there any reason at all why he should be accepted as a sage?

The love of God is the second most important requirement of salvation after *Ma'rifat* [recognition of God]. No one wishes to chastise the one who loves him; and love actually draws love. When you truly love someone, he cannot be averse to you. Even if you do not express it, your love will still have an effect and the beloved will, at the very least, not hate you. This is why it is said, 'A heart always finds its way to a heart.'[34] The reason why God's Prophets and Messengers have such a powerful attraction that thousands of people are drawn to them, and love them, and are ready to lay down their very lives for them, is that their own hearts are filled with great love and compassion for mankind, and their love exceeds even the love of a mother, and they desire the welfare of mankind even at the cost of their own suffering. Their true love, therefore, draws the fortunate hearts towards them.

If man, despite being ignorant of the unseen, can some-

---

[34] Literal translation of the Urdu proverb *'Dil ko dil se rah hoti hai.'* [Publishers]

how learn about the hidden love someone has for him, why cannot God, Who is All-Knowing, learn about a man's true love for Him? Love is a wonderful thing. Its fire consumes the fire of sin and extinguishes the flame of disobedience. There can be no question of 'punishment' where there is perfect and true love. One of the signs of true love is that the lover dreads the very thought of being estranged from his beloved. He thinks himself doomed at his smallest fault, and sees the beloved's displeasure as a deadly poison. He is also beset by a great longing to meet his beloved, and absence and separation takes the very life out of him. That is why he does not only regard as sinful, actions which are regarded as such by the common man— e.g., murder, adultery, theft and bearing false witness— rather, he considers even the slightest estrangement from God, and the slightest inclination towards anything other than Him, as a grave sin. He, therefore, constantly seeks forgiveness (*Istighfār*) from his Eternal Beloved. Since he can never bring himself to accept separation from Him at any time, the slightest neglect—which he might commit due to his human weakness—appears to him like a moun- tain of sin. It is for this reason that those who enjoy a holy and perfect relationship with God always occupy them- selves with *Istighfār*. A true lover is always apprehensive lest his beloved should become annoyed with him, and his heart is filled with the thirst to please Him perfectly, and he is not content even when God Himself informs him that He is pleased with him. Just as a drunkard is not satis- fied with drinking once and is constantly asking for more, in the same way, when the spring of Divine love gushes forth in a man's heart, he naturally wants to win God's pleasure as far as possible. Thus greater love leads to even greater *Istighfār*. This is why those who are perfect in their love for God are constantly seeking Allah's forgiveness, and the surest sign of a sinless person is that he occupies himself in *Istighfār* far more than other people. The true meaning of *Istighfār* is to pray to God that He may remove the possibility of any transgression or error which a person might commit due to the weakness of human nature, and that He may cover his faults and not allow them to be exposed. The meaning of *Istighfār* also extends to the common people, and, in their case, it means: to pray to God that He may protect the supplicant from evil consequences and poisonous influences of his transgressions and misdeeds, both in this world and the hereafter.

The source of true salvation, therefore, is personal love for God, which, in turn, draws His love through man's humility, supplication and constant *Istighfār*. When a person carries his love to perfection and the fire of love consumes his carnal passions, then, all at once, a flame of God's love—which He has for his servant—falls upon his heart and cleanses him of the dirt of his mundane existence. He then acquires the complexion of holiness of God, Who is *Ḥayyī* and *Qayyūm*, and partakes of all Divine attributes by way of reflection (*ẓill*). He then becomes a manifestation of Divine glory, and all that is hidden in God's eternal treasure is disclosed to the world through him. Since God—Who created this world—is not

Fountain of Christianity   **59**

a miser, and His blessings are everlasting, and His names
and attributes are never suspended, He grants to the people of the latter days the same bounties that He gave to
earlier people, but on the condition of piety and effort.
This is in keeping with the prayer which He has taught us
in the Holy Quran:

اِهْدِنَا الصِّرَاطَ الْمُسْتَقِيْمَ ۬ صِرَاطَ الَّذِيْنَ اَنْعَمْتَ عَلَيْهِمْ 35

That is, O Lord, show us the right path; the path of those
who received Your gifts and favours, i.e., O Lord, give us
the same rewards and bounties which You gave to the
Prophets and *Ṣiddīqīn* [those who testified to the truth],
and do not withhold any of Your gifts from us.

This verse holds out for this umma a great promise which
distinguishes it from all past ummas. All the Prophets of
the past possessed diverse excellences and they were
granted various blessings and bounties, but God has commanded us to pray that all those excellences may be given
to us. And it is obvious that when all those diverse qualities and excellences come together, they will become far
more impressive. That is why it has been said,
كُنْتُمْ خَيْرَ اُمَّةٍ اُخْرِجَتْ لِلنَّاسِ 36, i.e., On account of your excellences, you are the best of all peoples.

The reason why God has promised to bring together all
the various excellences into this umma, is because our
Holy Prophet[sa] himself embodies all the excellences. God

---

35 Al-Fātiḥah, 1:6-7 [Publishers]
36 Āl-e-ʻImrān, 3:111 [Publishers]

60   **Fountain of Christianity**

says in the Holy Quran [37]فَبِهُدٰىهُمُ اقْتَدِهْ i.e., 'Follow all the teachings that were given to all the Prophets.' The person who embodies all these teachings will, of course, be greater than all the Prophets, and anyone who follows such a Prophet will also acquire all these excellences by way of reflection (*zill*). Therefore, the purpose of teaching this prayer in *Sūrah Al-Fātiḥah* is that the perfect believers of the umma, who follow this perfect Prophet[sa], may also acquire all these excellences. I feel sorry for those who think that this umma is dead. How can they prefer to remain dead when God has taught them to pray for all excellences! It is a grievous sin in their eyes if someone claims, for instance, that he receives revelation like the Messiah, son of Mary[as],[38] and they consider such a person

---

[37] Al-An'ām, 6:91 [Publishers]

[38] These so called maulawis virtually insult our lord and master Muhammad[sa]—the best of Prophets and most exalted of Messengers— when they say that no one resembling Jesus[as], son of Mary, can ever appear in this umma, and that, because of this prohibition, God will have to break the seal of *Khatm-e-Nubuwwat* [Finality of Prophethood] and bring back the same Israelite Jesus into the world once more. Thus they stand guilty of, not one, but two sins. (1) First, they have to believe that while a servant of God named Jesus—or Yesu in Hebrew—attained closeness to God and became a Prophet by following the Mosaic law for thirty years, but in the case of the Holy Prophet[sa], no one can attain the same spiritual station even if he follows him for fifty years, instead of thirty. In other words, they say that no honour can be attained by following the Holy Prophet[sa]. They do not realize that this belief implies that God is only deceiving people by teaching them the prayer صِرَاطَ الَّذِيْنَ اَنْعَمْتَ عَلَيْهِمْ They also believe that, by virtue of his second coming, Jesus[as] is *Khātam-ul-Anbiyā'* [the last Prophet] as well as the last Judge and Arbiter. They do not understand the true meaning of this prophecy, which is that, since there will be people in this umma who Contd...

Fountain of Christianity 61

to be a kafir because they believe the door of Divine con-

will be like the Jews, God will send to them someone who would be the like of Jesus[as], and he will be an *ummatī* [follower of the Holy Prophet[sa]] as well as a Prophet. Jesus[as], son of Mary, cannot claim both these titles, for an *ummatī* is he who attains spiritual exaltation by submitting to the Prophet whom he follows, but Jesus[as] will already be in possession of this excellence. (2) Their other sin is that they believe Jesus[as] to be alive. This is in contrast to the categorical statement of the Holy Quran, which says:

فَلَمَّا تَوَفَّيۡتَنِیۡ کُنۡتَ اَنۡتَ الرَّقِیۡبَ عَلَیۡهِمۡ**

They interpret this verse to mean, 'When You raised me to heaven in my physical body...' It is a strange interpretation that only applies to Jesus[as]! The Holy Quran clearly states that this question will be put to Jesus[as] on the Day of Judgement, therefore, according to their interpretation of the word تَوَفَّیۡتَ it has to be believed that Jesus[as] will not have died prior to his appearance before God on the Day of Judgement. And if the verse فَلَمَّا تَوَفَّیۡتَنِیۡ is taken to mean, 'How could I have ever known about the condition of my people after You had caused me to die?', this interpretation would also be wrong in the context of their belief, for God would reply: "Why are you lying to Me that you do not know about the condition of your people, while you have been to the world a second time and have stayed there for forty years, and have waged wars against the Christians and have broken the cross?" Another thing that follows from their interpretation is that the Christians have not gone astray and are still on the right path because Jesus[as] is still alive in heaven! They should really die of shame!

In conclusion, remember that the 'Seal of Prophethood' does not break if a follower of the Holy Prophet[sa] is honoured with revelation, inspiration and Prophethood, and is even given the title of 'Prophet' through obedience to him, for such a person is only a follower and is nothing in himself. All his excellence is, in fact, the excellence of the Prophet whom he follows. And he is not called a Prophet, but a Prophet and a follower. But the coming back of a Prophet, who is not a follower, will surely go against *Khatm-e-Nubuwwat*. [Author]

* [Guide us on] the path of those on whom You have bestowed Your favours.—Al-Fātiḥah, 1:6 [Publishers]

** But since Thou didst cause me to die, Thou hast been the Watcher over them—Al-Mā'idah, 5:118 [Publishers] verse to have been closed to the Day of Judgement. Strangely enough, although they believe that God still hears as He did in the past, they do not believe that He also speaks in the same manner. If He does not speak in this age, then it is impossible to prove that He hears. These are extremely unfortunate people who believe God's attributes to have been suspended, and they are the real enemies of Islam. Their interpretation of *Khatm-e-Nubuwwat* [Seal of Prophethood] is a negation of Prophethood itself. Can we take *Khatm-e-Nubuwwat* to mean that all the blessings that could result from obedience to the Holy Prophet[sa] have now been barred, and that it is now futile to wish for Divine converse and dialogue? لَعۡنَةُ اللّٰهِ عَلَى الۡكَاذِبِيۡنَ [39] If this is true, can they tell us what then is the use of following the Holy Prophet[sa]? Dead is the religion which possesses only past tales and dead is the religion for which the path to Divine recognition has been closed. But Islam is a living religion. The Holy Quran, in *Sūrah Al-Fātiḥah*, declares Muslims to be the heirs to the excellences of all past Prophets, and it teaches them to pray for all the bounties that were given to them. Those who possess only tales of the past cannot be the heirs to these bounties. It is indeed a great pity that the fountain of all blessings has been made to flow before them, but they do not wish to drink even a little out of it!

Returning to the subject under discussion, let me repeat

---

[39] May Allah's curse be upon those who lie. [Publishers]

Fountain of Christianity　　　　　　　　　　　　　　　**63**

that love and recognition of God is the true source of salvation. As one progresses in *Ma'rifat*, so does he progress in Divine love, for beauty and benevolence are the two things that inspire love. When man learns about the beauty and benevolence of God, and sees how beautiful He is on account of His innumerable excellences, and realizes how he is overwhelmed by His unending kindness, all this causes his love for God—which has been eternally ingrained in his nature—to gush forth. And since God possesses the greatest beauty and excellence, and is constantly Benevolent and Bounteous, His seeker, having recognized these qualities, loves Him with such a love that he considers none to be equal to Him.[40] He then testifies to His being One, not just verbally, but in practice also, and he falls in love with His beauty and His holy attributes. Although the seed of Divine love is an eternal part of man's nature, it only blossoms when it is watered

---

[40] True *Ma'rifat* [recognition of God], as I have repeatedly stated, cannot be attained without Divine revelation and communion, and without the extraordinary signs that accompany Divine revelation and reveal God's Divinity and Power. This is the kind of Divine recognition which seekers hunger and thirst for, and without which they are as good as dead. Now, do you really think that Islam does not provide this *Ma'rifat* and that it is only a dead religion? *لَعْنَةُ اللهِ عَلَى الْكَاذِبِينَ   Nay, Islam is the only living faith which gives life to its followers. It is the only faith which shows God to us in this very world, and it is only through its blessings that I myself receive Divine revelations and am able to show great signs. All the other faiths of the world are dead; they possess no blessings, no life; they cannot grant us conversation with God, and we cannot witness God's miraculous work through them. Will anyone compete with us in these blessings? [Author]
* May Allah's curse be upon the liars! [Publishers]

with *Ma'rifat*. A lover cannot be attracted to the beloved unless he recognizes him and sees the manifestation of his splendour and beauty and experiences his nearness. Only after a person has attained complete *Ma'rifat* does a radiant spark of Divine love fall upon his heart which pulls him towards God. Human soul then falls upon the threshold of the Eternal Beloved with all the humility of a lover. It plunges into the shoreless ocean of Divine Oneness and becomes so clean and pure that it is purged of all worldly filth and undergoes a glorious transformation. It then hates impurity just as God hates it, and God's will and God's pleasure becomes its will and its pleasure.

But, as I have already said, before this higher kind of love can be excited, the spiritual traveller who seeks God should become fully cognizant of His beauty and benevolence; and it should be fully impressed upon his heart and mind that God possesses unlimited excellences and infinite charm and beauty, and that it is impossible to imagine greater favours than those which He bestows and is forever ready to bestow on us. God be thanked that He has equipped this umma with everything necessary for attaining His perfect *Ma'rifat*, and we do not feel any embarrassment when we praise Him.[41]

---

[41] How embarrassed must a Christian feel when he says that God once died for three days. And how his own conscience must rebuke him, "Does God ever die?" If God has died once, is there anything to stop Him from dying again? Indeed, there is nothing to prove that such a 'God' is still alive. He might already be dead for all we know, because we do not find in Him any Contd...

Fountain of Christianity 65

We believe that all conceivable powers and excellences are to be found in the person and attributes of God Almighty. We do not believe, like the Āryas, that He does not have the power to create particles or souls, nor do we say—God forbid—that He is a miser and does not want to grant everlasting salvation to anyone; nor do we believe that He does not have the power and authority to grant salvation. Unlike the Ārya Samājists, we do not say that God has forever closed the door to revelation, nor do we say that He is hard-hearted and does not accept people's repentance and keeps subjecting them to millions of reincarnations as a recompense for a single sin, nor do we believe that He does not have the power to accept repentance.

We also do not believe, as the Christians do, that 'God' suffered death at one time, that he was arrested, imprisoned and put on the cross by the Jews, and that he was born of a woman, and even had brothers. We do not say that God went to Hell for three days in order to atone for people's sins, and that he could not grant them salvation without first dying for their sake and spending three days in Hell. Unlike the Christians, we do not believe that Divine revelation has been sealed after our Holy Prophet[sa], and that the door to Divine converse and communion is

---

signs of the living; He neither responds to those who call Him, nor does He show any miraculous work. Be sure, therefore, that their 'God' is dead and he lies buried in Mohallah Khānyār, Srinagar.

As for the Āryas, their souls have no God at all, for they consider these souls to be eternal and self-existing. [Author]

66   **Fountain of Christianity**

forever closed, for in *Sūrah Al-Fātiḥah* God has declared us to be the heirs to all the excellences of past Prophets and has called us 'the Best of Ummas'. There is no doubt that we have been granted greater faith in God's beauty and benevolence—which is the fountainhead of love— than anyone else. The most ignorant and unfortunate among the Muslims are those who do not believe in His perfect beauty and benevolence. On the one hand, they tarnish the concept of God's Oneness by declaring His creatures to be partners in His special attributes,[42] and

---

[42] Muslims, particularly the Ahl-i-Ḥadīth, profess strong faith in *Tauḥīd*, but, unfortunately, their condition fits the proverb, 'Spitting the gnat and swallowing the camel'. Can we really call them believers in the Unity of God when they believe Jesus[as] to be one and without partner, just like God is, and when they believe that he went to heaven in his physical body and will return to earth some day, and that he is the one who created the birds! The unbelievers repeatedly swore that if the Holy Prophet[sa] could only ascend to heaven in his physical body, they would at once accept him, but the answer given to them was ***** قُلْ سُبْحَانَ رَبِّیْ هَلْ كُنْتُ اِلَّا بَشَرًا رَّسُوْلًا i.e., tell them, my Lord never breaks His word, and I cannot go to heaven because He has promised ****** فِیْهَا تَحْیَوْنَ وَفِیْهَا تَمُوْتُوْنَ and ******* وَلَكُمْ فِی الْاَرْضِ مُسْتَقَرٌّ Are we to believe that God forgot this promise when He took Jesus to heaven, or are we to assume that Jesus was not a mortal at all? If Jesus did go to heaven in his physical body, it would inevitably follow, in the light of the Quranic statement, that he was not a human being. What is more, these so-called advocates of Islam have attributed even to the Dajjāl qualities which necessarily make him God. What a pity that they should profess *Tauḥīd* and yet make such claims! [Author]

* Banī Isrā'īl, 17:94 [Publishers]

** Therein shall you live, and therein shall you die.—Al-A'rāf, 7:26
[Publishers]

*** And for you there is an abode on the earth.—Al-A'rāf, 7:25
[Publishers]

Fountain of Christianity   **67**

thus substitute the luminous beauty of His Oneness with the darkness of 'associating partners with Him'; and, on the other hand, they consider themselves deprived of the Holy Prophet's[sa] eternal bounty, as though—God forbid— he were not a 'living lamp', but a dead one that cannot light other 'lamps'. They believe that Moses[as] was a 'living lamp' that lit up hundreds of other 'lamps' in the form of Prophets, and that the Messiah was honoured with Prophethood because he followed the Shariah of Moses[as] and commandments of the Torah for thirty years, but they do not believe that anyone can gain spiritual merit by fol- lowing the Holy Prophet[sa]! They believe that he was not only deprived of a male issue—who would serve as his physical heir, as mentioned in the verse

$$\text{مَا كَانَ مُحَمَّدٌ اَبَآ اَحَدٍ مِّنْ رِّجَالِكُمْ}^{43}$$

but that he was also deprived of spiritual offsprings who would inherit his spiritual excellences. Thus they consider God's words

$$\text{وَلٰكِنْ رَّسُوْلَ اللّٰهِ وَخَاتَمَ النَّبِيّٖنَ}^{44}$$

to be meaningless. Here the Arabic word *lākin* (but) has obviously been used as a word of rectification, which speaks of the fulfilment in a different form of something that has hitherto remained unfulfilled. In this context, the

---

43 Muhammad is not the father of any of your men.—Al-Aḥzāb, 33:41 [Publishers]
44 But *he is* the Messenger of Allah and the Seal of the Prophets.—Al-Aḥzāb, 33:41 [Publishers]

verse means that, though the Holy Prophet[sa] did not have any male offspring, he will have countless spiritual progeny, and that he is 'the Seal of Prophets', which means that no one will attain the excellence of Prophethood unless he possesses the certificate of obedience to him. This is the true connotation of this verse, but these people have completely reversed its meaning and have rejected the bounty of Prohethoood in the future, even though this implies a criticism of the Holy Prophet[sa] himself. The perfection of a Prophet lies in his ability to impart to his followers the excellence of Prophethood by way of reflection (*zill*), and to give them complete spiritual nourishment, and it is for this purpose that Prophets are sent. Like mothers, they take into their lap the seekers after truth and feed them the 'milk' of Divine recognition. If the Holy Prophet[sa] did not possess this 'milk', then we will have to say—God forbid—that there is nothing to prove his Prophethood. But this is not at all true, for the Holy Quran calls him *Sirāj-e-Munīr* (the Radiant Lamp), which gives light to others and, through its influence, makes them like itself. If—God forbid—the Holy Prophet[sa] did not possess any spiritual influence, there would be no point in his coming, and God Himself would be considered a deceiver, because He taught the people to pray for the excellences of all the Prophets but He never had the intention of granting these excellences, and He always wished to keep them in the dark.

Remember, O Muslims! It is the height of ignorance and stupidity to harbour this belief. If Islam is indeed such a 'dead' religion, then whom will you invite to embrace it?

Will you take its corpse to Japan or will you offer it to Europe? Who would be foolish enough to fall for a 'dead' religion which, when compared to older religions, is found to be without any blessings and spirituality? In those religions, even women—such as Moses[as]' mother and Mary[as]—have received Divine revelations, but even your men cannot equal them!

The fact, O naïve and blind people, is that our Holy Prophet[sa], and our lord and master, (countless blessings be upon him), surpassed all Prophets in his spiritual influence. The influence of all past Prophets came to an end at a certain point and their people and their religions have no trace of life left in them, but the spiritual influence of the Holy Prophet[sa] will endure to the Last Day. For this reason, this umma does not require that a Messiah should come into it from outside; for, under the Holy Prophet's[sa] benign influence, even an ordinary man can become a Messiah, just as God has done in my case.

Let me now return to the original discussion and state the philosophy behind the Islamic concept of salvation. While, on the one hand, there has been placed in man's nature a poison which eternally draws him towards sin, at the same time his nature has also been endowed with an antidote for this poison, which is the love of God. Both these forces have continued to influence man ever since his creation. The poisonous influence leads him towards chastisement, but the antidote, which is the power of Divine love, consumes all the sins as fire consumes straw. It is wrong to think that while the faculty of sin was present in his nature from eternity, the means of deliverance were only provided a short time ago after Jesus' crucifixion. Only a mindless person would accept such a doctrine. The truth is that both these faculties have been placed in man's nature from his very inception. It cannot be that God placed in human nature the inclination towards sin, but He forgot to provide him the means of salvation and this only occurred to him four thousand years later!

Concluding the subject, let me advise you in the name of God, that if you are really in search of the living blessings, then stop looking towards the Messiah who has long been dead and none of whose blessings live on to this today. His people, instead of being inebriated with the love of God, have exceeded every other people in being intoxicated with wine, and, instead of seeking the heavenly treasure, they crave for the riches of the world even if they have to get them through gambling. Instead, I invite you into the fold of the Muhammadi Messiah, who is اِمَامُكُمْ مِنْكُمْ and who offers fresh blessings. The choice is yours.

The Author
Mirza Ghulam Ahmad of Qadian,
The Promised Messiah

Supplication to God, the Glorious

O You, for Whom I would sacrifice my life,
My heart, and every particle of my being!
With Your mercy, open for me
All the paths to recognizing You.

The philosopher who seeks You
Through reason, is insane;
The hidden path that leads to You
Lies far from reason's domain.

None of them ever found
Your Holy Abode;
Only through Your limitless Grace
Has anyone ever found the Road.

You give both the worlds
To the lovers of Your Countenance;
But the two worlds are nothing
In the eyes of Your servants.

With just one look
Stop all this war and confrontation;
The world truly needs
A sign of Your manifestation.

Show a sign
So that the world may be filled with Your Light;
And every denier of the Faith
May sing Your praises day and night.

I would not be the least troubled
If the whole world was to turn upside down;
I am only worried lest Your Luminous Path
Should become lost and unknown.

Nothing comes out of religious debates
Put an end to them with Your Mighty signs.

Stir people's consciences with earthquakes
So that fear may bring them to Your Gates.

In the garb of an earthquake
Make a fountain of mercy flow;
How long will Your wailing servant
Languish in his sorrow?

Index of Quranic Verses

Ref.	Verse	Page
1:6-7	اِهۡدِنَا الصِّرَاطَ الۡمُسۡتَقِيۡمَ ۞ صِرَاطَ الَّذِيۡنَ اَنۡعَمۡتَ عَلَيۡهِمۡ	27,40,59,60
2:201	فَاذۡكُرُوا اللّٰهَ كَذِكۡرِكُمۡ اٰبَآءَكُمۡ	53
3:56	مُتَوَفِّيۡكَ	61
3:111	كُنۡتُمۡ خَيۡرَ اُمَّةٍ اُخۡرِجَتۡ لِلنَّاسِ	59
5:118	فَلَمَّا تَوَفَّيۡتَنِيۡ كُنۡتَ اَنۡتَ الرَّقِيۡبَ عَلَيۡهِمۡ	15,61
6:91	فَبِهُدٰىهُمُ اقۡتَدِهۡ	60
7:25	وَلَكُمۡ فِى الۡاَرۡضِ مُسۡتَقَرٌّ	66
7:26	فِيۡهَا تَحۡيَوۡنَ وَفِيۡهَا تَمُوۡتُوۡنَ	66
7:173	اَلَسۡتُ بِرَبِّكُمۡ قَالُوۡا بَلٰى	38
11:108	اِلَّا مَا شَآءَ رَبُّكَ اِنَّ رَبَّكَ فَعَّالٌ لِّمَا يُرِيۡدُ	45
17:94	قُلۡ سُبۡحَانَ رَبِّيۡ هَلۡ كُنۡتُ اِلَّا بَشَرًا رَّسُوۡلًا	15,66
20:75	اِنَّهٗ مَنۡ يَّأۡتِ رَبَّهٗ مُجۡرِمًا فَاِنَّ لَهٗ جَهَنَّمَ لَا يَمُوۡتُ فِيۡهَا وَلَا يَحۡيٰى	42
30:31	فِطۡرَتَ اللّٰهِ الَّتِيۡ فَطَرَ النَّاسَ عَلَيۡهَا	39
33:41	مَا كَانَ مُحَمَّدٌ اَبَآ اَحَدٍ مِّنۡ رِّجَالِكُمۡ وَلٰكِنۡ رَّسُوۡلَ اللّٰهِ وَخَاتَمَ النَّبِيّٖنَ	67
42:41	جَزٰٓؤُا سَيِّئَةٍ سَيِّئَةٌ مِّثۡلُهَا فَمَنۡ عَفَا وَاَصۡلَحَ فَاَجۡرُهٗ عَلَى اللّٰهِ	16
55:30	كُلَّ يَوۡمٍ هُوَ فِيۡ شَأۡنٍ	46

Name and Subject Index

A

Aaron, the brother of Mary[as], 27, 29
Adam[as], 29
Ahl-i-Ḥadīth, 66
Ārya Samājists, 38, 47; attribute shortcomings to God, 48; believe souls and
particles to be eternal and self-existing, 49
Aṣḥāb-e-Kahf (the Companions of the Cave), 29

B

Bānsbareilly, 3
Baqā Billāh, 40
Barnabas, the Gospel of: contains a prophecy about the Holy Prophet[sa], 10
Buddha: Gospels allegedly copied the teachings of, 9; thought by some to be the
author of the Book of Yūz Āsaf, 9
Bukhārī, Ṣaḥīḥ, 4

C

Christianity, 3, 14, 19, 54; is the religion of Saint Paul, 52
Christians: attribute shortcomings to God, 48; have set a seal on all Divine
revelation, 19; interpolated their books, 7

D

Damascus: 'Pauline Trinity' was born in, 54; prophecy about the Promised Messiah
descending in the East of, 55; Qadian is located exactly to the East of, 55

E

Earthquakes, 17, 48
Edward, King, 10
Elijah[as]: showed greater miracles than Jesus[as], 14; was supposed to return before the
coming of the Messiah, 20, 31

F

Fanā Fillāh, 40

G

God Almighty: Attributes of, 17, 24, 45, 46, 62, 63, 66; are never suspended, 59;
Ḥayyī, 36; Omnipotence, 35; Omniscience, 35; Oneness, 35; *Qayyūm*, 36; hears
and speaks even in this age, 23; Holy Quran practically proves the existence of,

Index   **75**

23; is not only forbearing but also severe in His wrath, 17; recognition of (*Ma'rifat*), 42, 48, 56, 63, 64; seeking forgiveness from. *See Istighfār*; there should be harmony between the word and action of, 17

Gospels, the, 10; allegedly copied from Buddhist teachings, 9; allegedly pirated from Jewish scriptures, 8; authenticity based on presumption and conjecture, not concrete evidence, 10; full of passages from Talmud and the Old Testament, 30; marked discrepancies between, 10

H

Hadith, 4, 44, 45, 55
Hell, 19, 24, 41, 65; all people will one day be freed from, 44

I

India: Jesus[as] travelled to, 9, 10, 15
Islam: continues to yield fresh blessings, 5; leads to the Living God, 5
Istighfār, 57, 58

J

James, brother of Jesus[as]: Jesus' successor and a holy man, 54; opposed by Saint Paul, 52
Jesus[as], 4; died and was buried in Kashmir, 5, 9, 14; Elijah[as] showed greater miracles than, 14; survived the cross and fled to Kashmir, 14; travelled to India, 9, 10, 15
Jews, 4, 12, 14, 15, 18, 19, 20, 24, 29, 31, 50, 54, 61, 65; do not believe that Jesus[as] showed any miracles, 14
Jonah[as], 31
Joseph the husband of Mary[as], 28

K

Kashmir: Jesus[as] died and was buried in, 5, 9, 14
Khatm-e-Nubuwwat (Finality of Prophethood), 60, 61, 62

L

London, 10
Lot[as], 17

M

Ma'rifat. See God Almighty, recognition of
Malachi, the book of, 20, 31
Manṣūrī Hills, 48
Marham-e-'Īsa (Jesus' Ointment), 32

76   **Index**

Mary[as], 28, 54, 60, 69; was the sister of Aaron, 27

Miracle/Miracles: more than three thousand shown by the Holy Prophet[sa], 22; more were shown by the Promised Messiah[as] than by Jesus[as], 26; of Elijah[as] were greater than those of Jesus[as], 14; of the Holy Prophet[sa] live on to this day, 22; of the Promised Messiah[as], 26; the Holy Quran proclaims itself a, 12

Mīzān-ul-Ḥaq, 12

Moses[as], 8, 50, 67, 69; mother of; was a recipient of Divine revelation, 69

Muhammad, the Holy Prophet[sa], 4, 12, 20, 22, 25, 26, 27, 30, 59, 60, 61, 62, 65, 66, 67, 68, 69; his miracles live on to this day, 22; one can attain a higher status than Jesus[as] by following, 26; showed more than three thousand miracles and made countless prophecies, 22; surpassed all Prophets in spiritual influence, 69

N

Neug, 47

Noah[as], 17

P

Paradise, 14, 24

Paul, Saint, 11, 52, 53, 54, 55; Christianity is the religion of, 52; introduced the doctrine of the Trinity, 51

Pfander, Reverend, 12

Polygamy, 28

Prayer, 59; acceptance of, 18; of Jesus[as] remained unanswered, 25

Promised Messiah[as], the: called a Kafir by the Mullahs, 3; conspiracies against, 25; God did not forsake, 25; granted thousands of signs and received Divine revelations almost every day, 22; honoured by God due to his complete obedience to the Holy Prophet[sa], 26; received greater Divine addresses than Jesus[as], 53; showed more miracles than Jesus[as], 26; was honoured due to his complete obedience to the Holy Prophet[sa], 26

Prophecy/Prophecies, 12, 14, 55; about the Holy Prophet[sa] found in the Gospel of Barnabas, 10; the Holy Prophet[sa] made countless, 22

Q

Qadian: is located exactly to the East of Damascus, 55

Quran, the Holy, 4, 10, 11, 12, 13, 15, 16, 21, 22, 26, 27, 29, 30, 34, 38, 41, 51, 59, 60, 61, 62, 68; accused of copying from past scriptures, 8; consists only of Divine revelation, 13, 31; does not teach that the sinners will live in Hell forever, 44; has done a favour to Jesus[as] by affirming his Prophethood, 31; nourishes all the human faculties, 16; practically proves the existence of God, 23; proclaims itself to be a miracle, 12; reflects the Divine law of nature, 17; rejects the concept of the Trinity, 50; teaches both forgiveness and retribution, 15; Torah teaches the Unity of God just like, 51

Index   77

R

Raf'a (Ascension), true meaning of, 49
Repentance, 18, 65
Revelation, Divine: cannot be criticized because of similarity to past scriptures, 21;
   Christians have set a seal on, 19; does not need to borrow from other books, 30;
   Islam has not closed the door to, 22, 26, 65; received by women, 69; the Quran
   contains only, 13, 31; truth or falsity of a scripture can only be established
   through, 11

S

Sale, George, 11
Salvation, 33, 38, 39, 40, 41, 42, 43, 44, 45, 46, 47, 48, 49, 56, 58, 63, 65, 69, 70
Sanskrit, 9
Swine, flesh of, 52, 54, 55

T

Talmud: Gospel teachings allegedly copied from, 8, 30
Trimurti, Hindu doctrine of, 51
Trinity, the doctrine of the, 18, 50, 51, 52, 54, 55

V

Vedas, 11, 47

Y

Yanābī-ul-Islam, 3, 5, 7; claims that the Quran has been copied from past accounts,
   8
Yūz Āsaf, the book of: believed by some to be the book of Buddha, 9; Gospels are
   said to have been copied from, 9; Jesus' own Gospel, 9

Z

Zill, 41, 58, 60, 68